PRAYER

PRAYER
LANGUAGE
OF THE
SOUL

PHILIP DUNN

Daybreak™ Books
An Imprint of Rodale Books
New York, New York

Printed in the United States of America on acid-free ∞ , recycled paper ♻
Cover Designer: Barbara Scott-Goodman
Book Designer: Eugenie S. Delaney

Library of Congress Cataloging-in-Publication Data

Lorie, Peter.
    Prayer : language of the soul / Philip Dunn.
        p.   cm.
    Includes index.
    ISBN 0–87596–428–1 hardcover
    1. Prayer. 2. Prayers. I. Title.
    BL560.L66 1997
    291.4'3—dc21   97–13472

Distributed in the book trade by St. Martin's Press

2 4 6 8 10 9 7 5 3 1   hardcover

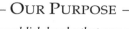

OUR PURPOSE

*"We publish books that empower
people's minds and spirits."*

To my gracious and loving parents
Gordon and Gwen

᪉

CONTENTS

ɔ

ACKNOWLEDGMENTS

The author would like to thank the following for their help in making this book possible: Chris Tomasino, for starting the whole story, and I mean the whole story! Karen Kelly for her feedback and energy. Silent Unity and Agape for their willing help and for the work they do on behalf of all of us.

Grateful acknowledgment is also made to the authors and publishers for use of their material. Every effort has been made to contact original sources.

INTRODUCTION

⁊

Most people consider the course of events as natural and inevitable.
They little know what radical changes are possible through prayer.
PARAMAHANSA YOGANANDA

URING A TIME IN INDIA, WHILE VISITING AN ASHRAM south of Bombay, I sat before a spiritual teacher who had been working with westerners from the United States and Europe, most of whom had come to him for the same reasons I was there— some form of search for the inner life. He had instructed many individuals in meditation and prayer, and during our conversation he asked me if I knew what prayer was. I hesitated, trying to formulate an intelligible answer, something I supposed might impress him with my virtues, virtues that I imagined then might be appropriate to someone I undoubtedly considered my superior in such matters. What was prayer? What was prayer for me? What could prayer be for others in my world, or any world for that matter? Nothing came. He remained silently waiting for my response. Perhaps prayer was contemplation. Perhaps it was a silent awareness of truth. Perhaps it was a mystical value that eluded me and had something to do with God, or silence or stillness. Somehow the words would not formulate into anything that could possibly make any sense, let alone make him feel that I was a good subject for his wisdom.

So without further ado I told him that I did not know what prayer was, but I knew what it wasn't. I felt that when I was thinking I wasn't praying. That when I was worrying I wasn't praying. I felt that when I was rushing around at high speed in my life as an achiever I probably wasn't praying either, and that in fact, come to think of it, pretty much everything I did in my life wasn't praying!

He smiled benevolently, exactly the way one would expect such a being to smile. It was as though a ray of approval had been cast over me, and despite my weaknesses and my lack of holiness, I had clearly told him exactly what he wanted to hear, or rather I had told him something that was acceptable to him. As a westerner in the presence of the most holy of individuals, I had found the best thing that western seekers like to find: divine approval; the summit, it seemed then, of achievement. And I had found it simply by being honest.

Not knowing what prayer was was the first step to learning and understanding what it is. Like Alcoholics Anonymous tells its students, the first thing you have to do in order to recover from alcoholism is to admit that you drink too much. I, as a student, or patient, seeking help from Achievers Anonymous, or Thinkers Anonymous, had past the first grade. I had admitted the sickness.

In fact, he went on to tell me that actually, all I needed to do to learn what prayer was was to realize that I was constantly in a state of prayer whether I knew it or not, and all the thinking and feeling, doubting and worrying was prayer—a certain type of prayer that is begging the divine existence around me to help me relax.

Please God, help me to stop worrying, chattering in my mind, and give me some relief from all these constant habits that prevent me from finding joy in my life—worry, worry, worry!

It became increasingly clear to me over the following years that everything is actually prayer of one sort or another, and that as we become more and more aware of this, so also we, in a manner of speaking, open up the gaps between the thoughts, fears, and doubts—gaps where silence exists—and allow a kind of divine intervention to happen that provides us with more and more space to be silent and still. Mankind has always, since the beginning of time, yearned for peace, for some sort of break from the moment-to-moment round of activities and troubles he envisages that his life is made from. "God, if only I could take a break!" "My God, I have so much to do, I think I'll never get a vacation!" "Jesus, when will I ever find some peace in all this?" Most of us have uttered such prayers on a constant basis during our lives, and if we finally reach a point where we are genuinely exhausted

by events, tired of the never-ending hassle of life, it is then that we
begin to revolt against it and look for the gaps that provide us with
deeper prayer and meditation.

Another way in which God, life, existence—whatever we wish to
call the divine—provides us with an opportunity to learn about prayer
is through disillusionment. Life has a habit of disappointing us over
and over again. We fail in our work, our relationships, and our
attempts to find happiness. Even when we are successful in these
things, we very often still feel like failures, as though life wants to
knock us on the head just for the sake of it.

> *He looked up at the sky*
> *And it rained on his head,*
> *So he looked down at the ground*
> *And a dog bit him.*
> *So he buried himself in his work*
> *And they fired him.*
> *So he took pills and died*
> *But they sent him back.*

These are simply opportunities for us to take another step forward,
and the most profound disillusionment is probably the most profound
state of potential learning, for if we finally become tired and
disillusioned with everything, we are forced one of two ways: death
(perhaps not physical but certainly psychological), depression, bitterness, doubt, cynicism—conditions that Western man is thoroughly familiar with, especially during old age. Or alternatively, transformation.

This book is not about having doubts, or about becoming
depressed, bitter, and cynical. It is hopefully an attempt to help toward
transformation. For prayer transforms.

It doesn't have to be dramatic transformation, though it can be. It
can also be very tender, partial, temporary, even fleeting. All this is
transformation, and it's a lot better than pain, bitterness, and sadness.

The following pages are made up of various guides for those who
know what prayer isn't as well as those who may know what it is, or

believe that they might. There is a history of prayer plus a series of sections on the different kinds of prayer that have been practiced by all the various formats of religiousness. This book is intended to entertain and enlighten those who are interested. There is some fairly healthy advice on what prayer can do for us, as even some scientists and doctors these days believe prayer to be a cure for many ills, both physical and psychological, and we already know what good it does for the spirit.

Then, there is the prayer section, with around 300 prayers ranging across all denominations and all times in history.

Finally there is a section providing addresses, telephone numbers, and e-mail and Web site addresses for locations that seem the most exciting and dramatic examples of how prayer can be used to generate joy in the world. This includes selected locations for Christian, Buddhist, Hindu, Judaic, Native American, Shamanic, Wiccan, Sufi, and non- and trans-denominational centers throughout the United States. In this section there are also a number of addresses for organizations and institutions that seem relevant to prayer in the United States plus an international section for travelers.

At the end of the book there is a first-line index to help find familiar prayers, a key-word index, and a directory of prayer sources. There is also a bibliography and reading list.

I hope that you enjoy the book and that if you still don't know what prayer is at the end of it, you will read it again!

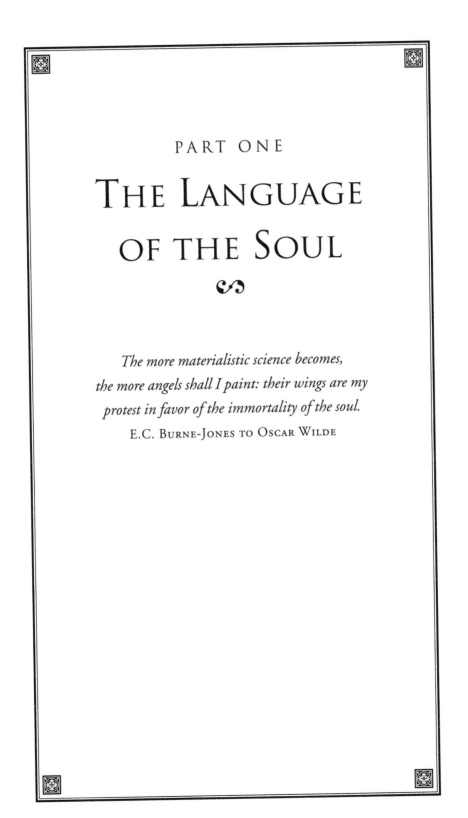

PART ONE

THE LANGUAGE
OF THE SOUL

ᏻ

*The more materialistic science becomes,
the more angels shall I paint: their wings are my
protest in favor of the immortality of the soul.*
E.C. BURNE-JONES TO OSCAR WILDE

WHY WE PRAY

કૈ

When the mind knows, we call it knowledge.
When the heart knows, we call it love.
When the being knows, we call it prayer.

ANONYMOUS

IN ITS EARLIEST INCARNATIONS PRAYER WAS A WAY OF LIFE
that occupied every hour of the day, not simply kneeling in
prayer, but as a fabric of life, in thought, in deed, and in relationship
with the world. Within the most ancient traditions, such as Vedism in
India, which developed into the Hindu faiths, and within Western
pagan religions, such as those of the pre-Christian Celts and Native
Americans, prayer was a connection to existence in the broadest sense,
a synergy with godliness, a part of mysticism. It was practiced as something that sprang from a simple place of silence and stillness, out of
which the one who prayed was inclined toward perfection and
absolute bliss. This, in its natural tranquillity, brought all that might
be wished for, but not necessarily in the form of some specific request
or the granting of a wish. The receipt of beauty, joy, and spiritual and
material wealth was the natural result of an understanding of the individual's connection with existence. This formation of prayer, in its
most profound shape, was also highly practical in its content and its
different silhouettes. The forefathers of our religiousness were
concerned not only with enlightenment of the highly evolved but also
with the day-to-day behavior of ordinary individuals and their hopes
for fulfillment.

A simple example of this concern was the prayer before meals.
Food needs to be digested by a body at peace. The hustle and bustle of
everyday life is not necessarily the best basis for enhancing the needs of
every cell that makes it function. A prayer breaks the pattern of activity and brings silence and peace to the meal, all the better to digest the
food and allow it to energize the body more thoroughly. Similarly, a

Vedism is the religion of the ancient Indo-European-speaking peoples who entered India about 1500 B.C.E. from the region of present-day Iran. Vedism takes its name from the collection of sacred texts known as the Vedas.

Vedism is the oldest stratum of religious activity in India for which there exist written materials. It was the starting point of Hinduism.

Vedism involved the worship of numerous male divinities who were connected with the sky and natural phenomena. The priests who officiated at this worship were known as Brahmans. The complex Vedic ceremonies, for which the hymns of the Rig-Veda were composed, centered on the ritual sacrifice of animals and with the pressing and drinking of a sacred, intoxicating liquor called soma. The basic Vedic rite was performed by offering these substances to a sacred fire, and this fire, which was itself deified as Agni, carried the oblations to the gods of the Vedic pantheon. The greatest deities of Vedism were at the same time material elements of the ritual offering: On the one hand, Agni (fire), which was equally the fire of the sun, of lightning, of burning wood, and of that which made light for the purpose of religious worship; and on the other hand, Soma, which was simply the deified aspect of the liquid poured in the oblation. The god of highest rank, however, was Indra, a warlike god who conquered innumerable human and demon enemies and vanquished the sun, among other epic feats. Another great deity was Varuna, who was the upholder of the cosmic and moral laws. Vedism had many other lesser deities, among whom were gods, demigods, and demons.

prayer before sleep helps curtail the anxieties of a busy day and prepare the body for a restful night.

Prayer and mysticism were in some part essentially related to the practical in their earliest inception. It has only been in recent centuries that the whole concept of religious behavior has passed almost totally into the realms of the mysterious and, therefore, to the specialist. Today our prayer tends to happen in formalized situations such as in church or at special meetings and gatherings of like-minded people. Prayer before going to sleep might help our conscience if we think there's a chance we won't wake up in the morning. We might pray because we want something: a raise, a lover, or better health. Prayer very often tends to arise less from a longing of the heart and soul and more from desire, and somehow desire appears to us not to work so well in our connection with God. Desires arise from the mind; longing is from the heart. It seems that the heart has a more profound contact with the mysteries of life.

In the past some of our religions have taught that we have little direct recourse to God, that we must talk to him through others who have been specially trained or anointed to be our intermediaries. This has also led us to doubt our ability to communicate with the divine, as though somehow we must act as the lower ranks in some hierarchy of understanding.

Prayer is a direct link with the universal, the total, the absolute. It does not connect with only the Christian, the Hindu, or the Islamic god. These are all imagined variations on a theme of existence that may help us to "connect," but which we do not need. Prayer connects us with life as god, regardless of religious persuasion. No one will be refused by life's god, for all those that long from their hearts to be heard by existence are heard and answered. In some ways we need to unlearn a lot of our more recent religious conditioning in order to fully communicate with life as god, as we will see in the pages of this book. Religiousness is a universal quality common to the source of all established and many new religions.

But there is one vital aspect of all this, a quality to prayer that is not always understood or accepted. We have discussed the difference between desire and longing—the difference being between the mind and the heart. We may believe that simply sitting or kneeling in prayer and repeating the words of a prayer is enough. We may "think" our prayers through habit, and in thinking the words, we may hope that they pass into existence and are granted in some way. Or we may also "feel" our prayers at a much deeper level, uttering them from the being, without need for hope or desire but with a simple willingness to allow the prayer to take its place in life, for life's god to absorb it. This would be the way to really engage with the prayers we utter, for it contains an element of acceptance and surrender to life. In fact, as alluded to in the introduction to this book, this latter prayer is what we actually do anyway, in a sort of unconscious communication with life that happens somewhere inside us—constantly asking, desiring, feeling, and thinking our prayers. And as we become more and more conscious and silent within ourselves—as we widen the gaps between the thoughts, so our prayers are better directed.

The Beginnings
of Prayer

HE VERY EARLIEST FORMAT FOR RELIGIOUS EXPRESSION WAS a natural and total part of the existence of life. Religion, in fact, was life. All rituals and processes for the fulfillment of daily routine arose out of religious feelings and rituals. The hunting for food, the planting and gathering of crops, and the survival in an often hazardous world were accompanied by deeply mystical and religious rituals. These practices arose out of a powerful sense of awe for life and the environment that contained it. Primitive tribes knew nothing of the science involved in the miraculous elements of their world. They were literally astonished at life in all its awesome beauty. They also felt and understood at a deep level their part in this miraculous world, for they recognized that life worked for them only when they behaved in certain ways. Their rules were related to natural phenomena and seasonal activity.

Religion, and therefore prayer as its expression, was the primary mode of communication with nature. In fact, it still is today, though we often are confused by the constant incursions of what appear to be conflicts and frictions brought about through the empirical data of science and rational education. We believe that we know what the sun, moon, and stars represent. We have a greater understanding of the superficial elements of life and therefore believe that we cannot any longer trust the unseen, unknowable forces that still surround us.

MYSTICISM
AND MAGIC
cx

*Mysticism is the art of union with reality. The mystic is a person
who has attained that union in greater degree or who aims at
and believes in such attainment.*

EVELYN UNDERHILL

*The most beautiful thing we can experience is the mysterious. It is the
source of all true art and science.*

ALBERT EINSTEIN

 EFORE WE GO FURTHER INTO HOW WE CAN PRAY IN THE
complex world we have invented, it is worth taking a few short
detours, the first of which is a closer look at how mysticism and
magic were recognized by our forefathers as a basis for life, for they
still exist as our foundations, though we are nowadays often somewhat
confused by them. We will also travel briefly through some of the
Eastern and Western expressions of mysticism before returning to the
underlying story of our need to pray.

It is recorded throughout our written history that prayer was associated, though not exclusively, with magic. The evolution of prayer is
often viewed today, however, as having grown independently of magic.
We have tended to consider magic in a different category from
religion, though in fact their paths have crossed perpetually. For example, the bodily positions—such as standing, kneeling, crouching, lying
prostrate, and bowing the head—and the position of the hands—such
as raised, outstretched, folded, crossed, or clasped—that are associated
with the act of prayer, were also mirrored in magical techniques
designed to protect against danger from some superhuman entity. As
far as history and reference books are concerned, religion and magic
are often represented as two separate things: one involved in the sacred

and the other involved in the profane. We think of superstition, for example, as somehow primitive and disassociated from religion, though in truth all religion is intertwined with superstitious belief. The Holy Cross, for instance, was born out of the ancient Celtic belief in trees as symbols of potency.

The problem that arises out of separating the magical, the mystical, and the religious is that we tend to lose touch with the more secret and deeply felt elements that magic and mysticism bring to religion, even though remnants of them still surface in modern-day practice. Roman

The Celtic tribes did not record their religious beliefs. The pre-Christian Celts themselves left no writings. Other than a few inscriptions, the principal sources of modern information about them are contemporary Greek and Latin writers, notably Poseidonius, Lucan, and the Roman emperor Julius Caesar. Insight can also be gleaned from the sagas and myths, particularly of Ireland and Wales, that were recorded by native Christian monks centuries later. Celtic myth is for the most part a collection of remnants, difficult to sort out. Roman writers such as Caesar made a great effort to syncretize the Gallic gods with their own. While a common Indo-European heritage did manifest itself in certain parallels between the two cultures, their contrasts were far more striking. Celtic theology and eschatology were pervaded by a spirit of animism and a dreamlike consciousness that bore little resemblance to the rather impersonal Roman state religion. Celtic worship centered upon the interplay of the "otherworld" or divine element with the land and the waters. Wells, springs, rivers, and hills were inhabited by guardian spirits, usually female, the names of which survive in many place names. The land itself was regarded anthropomorphically as feminine. The ocean, ruled by the god Manannán, was also, particularly in British and Irish cosmology, a force of great magic and mystery. The natural connection between man, animal, and plant life and the gods that inhabited them expressed itself clearly in this organization of the world.

Catholicism, for example, still employs some very powerful mystical elements in its religious observances. In southern European countries such as Spain and Italy, the Roman Catholic communities still perform much of their ritual religious life on the basis of the oldest and most magical techniques. To see these rituals as somehow negatively primitive is a denial of our most profound foundations.

In our far distant past, and in the earliest religions, the mystical, the magical, and the divine were all one and the same. In fact, mysticism and magic were the original forerunners of the religions that we hold so dear today.

THE MYSTERIOUS MYSTERY
OF MYSTICISM

ↄ

HE WORD *MYSTERIOUS* AND THE WORD *MYSTICISM* BOTH derive from the same root, *mysterion*, meaning to gather together for a secret ceremony. Mysticism, which is the source of all religion, is the study, basically, of that which can only be experienced and not known. Mysticism is a "heart art," or a "being art," not a "mind art." It is essentially nonrational as well as irrational. In other words, we literally cannot "think" mysticism.

Mysticism. There is clearly something "unthinkable," nonlogical, paradoxical, and unpredictable about the mystical phenomenon. As Zen Buddhist masters say, it is knowledge of the most adequate kind, only it cannot be expressed in words. If there is a mystery about mystical experience, it is something that it shares with life and consciousness. Mysticism, a form of living in depth, indicates that man, a meeting ground of various levels of reality, is more than one-dimensional. Mysticism is essentially the unknowable aspect of life, the ultimate secret of God.

The relationship of the religion of faith to mysticism is ambiguous, a mixture of respect and misgivings. Though mysticism may be associated with religion in our minds, it need not be. Also, the mystic often represents a type that the religious institution (that is, the church) does not and cannot produce and does not know what to do with if and when one appears. As William Ralph Inge, an English theologian, commented, "Institutionalism and mysticism have been uneasy bedfellows." Although mysticism has been the core of Hinduism and Buddhism, it has been little more than a minor strand—and, frequently, a disturbing element—in Judaism, Christianity, and Islam. As the sixteenth-century Italian political philosopher Niccolò Machiavelli noted of the thirteenth-century Christian monastic leaders Saint Francis and Saint Dominic, they had saved religion but destroyed the church.

Mysticism and magic. Mysticism shares a common world with magic, prayer, worship, and religion. Though there is an element of magic, psychism, and the occult in much of what passes for mysticism, it is not to be equated with a science of the unseen or with voices and visions. Powers of the occult (or siddhas) are viewed as real, but they can also be dangerous and are not of interest to genuine mystics, who have warned against their likely misuse. Nevertheless, mysticism and magic originally grew from the same source of life as a mystery, both godly and satanic in nature.

Prayer and worship have always formed part of mysticism, but only as a union with God, not as a separated system of asking or receiving in the rational sense. Both mysticism and magic follow similar routes to the divine through ritual and shared experience rather than a rational or scientific investigation.

We experience the unknowable often. Falling in love or the feeling we get watching the sun set over a beautiful horizon can never be effectively communicated in words or written down. We can share the experience with another at the time it occurs, but we cannot tell it in its full glory. At best we can write a poem or paint a canvas, but this will never equal the power and glory of the mystical experience, and there have been many in our past who have felt the incredible and awesome strength of the mystical divine—such as Jesus, Buddha, Mahavira, Moses—individuals who founded the religions that many follow today.

These are experiences that bring us closer to God in ourselves and our environment. It might be suggested even that this God is actually our lives—not merely *in* our lives, but *of* our lives, and that when we touch the unknowable, the mystical, we are being reunited with God in ourselves.

The word *religion* in fact derives from the Latin root *religere*, which means "reunite." It should be noticed perhaps that the word is *reunite*, not *unite*. In other words, we are already united; we just need to remember it. Our links with the ancient mystical formats of religion and, therefore, prayer, are so deeply rooted within us that we cannot deny them, even though much of modern life attempts to make us do this.

Jesus. Matthew places the birth of Jesus at least two years before Herod the Great's death late in 5 B.C.E. or early in 4 B.C.E. Luke connects Jesus' birth with a Roman census that, according to Josephus, occurred between the years 6 and 7 C.E. and caused a revolt against the governor Quirinius. Luke could be right about the census and wrong about the governor. The crucifixion under Pontius Pilate, prefect of Judaea, was probably between the years 29 and 30 C.E., but again, certainty is impossible. Like all the most powerful and enlightened religious leaders of our past, we do not really know that much about the individuality or character of Jesus, probably largely because in the higher states of spiritual growth, character and personality disappear altogether and leave a kind of simple mirror that only exposes the personality of the observer. Details are therefore mostly subjective.

Mahavira (Sanskrit: "Great Hero"), by name of Vardahama (599 to 527 B.C.E.), was last of the 24 Tirthankaras (Fully Enlightened Teachers) who founded Jainism and was the reformer of the Jaina sangha (religious order). The traditions of the two main Jaina sects record that Mahavira became a monk and followed an extreme ascetic life, attaining kevala-jñana, the highest knowledge. Teaching a doctrine of austerity, Mahavira advocated nonviolence, vegetarianism, and the acceptance of the "five real vows" of renunciation. He spent almost his entire life completely naked and without any form of possession, except for a bowl, which he begged with.

MOKSHA—LIFE BEYOND HEAVEN AND HELL

❧

*T*HE FOUNDATIONS OF RELIGIOUSNESS IN THE MYSTICAL CAN be seen in many of the Hindu faiths today, which do not center on any single monotheistic god, but are concerned with the irrational, the ritualistic processes of divinity and meditation as a form of prayer, and ultimately what Hinduism calls Moksha. It is useful to learn about Moksha, as it offers a fascinating alternative description of what we are searching for in our need to reunite with the basic foundations of prayer and our connections with God.

Christian, Judaic, and Islamic faiths give two basic choices: heaven and hell. The whole foundation of our prayers, therefore, even in everyday life, is to avoid hell and find heaven. We can see this in all sorts of forms: how we eat, how we choose our work, and how we conduct our physical and psychological lives every minute of every day. And we often fail to succeed in our quest for heaven and find ourselves in hell instead, as if by accident or lack of understanding. The original and highly mystical foundation of heaven and hell was bound up in a deep longing for goodness and joy, as opposed to evil and sadness. Heaven was and, for many of us, still is, a fabulous tapestry of all the things that we most wish for ourselves and others, and hell was and is still, therefore, the alternative. But with the modern stresses and strains of life, we may lose sight of the mysticism and beauty of this ancient tradition and become caught up in the differences between the two rather than the power of them both as one whole aspect of life. Moksha provides an alternative way of looking at this completeness of good and evil in one belief.

For the Hindu, Moksha is a third choice. Heaven and hell are seen as temporary affairs. Certainly, we are going to be unhappy sometimes, and therefore in hell. For sure, we will sometimes be happy—in heaven—but ultimately, the Hindu wishes to be rid of both these al-

The god of heaven. God is often viewed as an ever-active father of the family, called upon but rarely the recipient of sacrifices. He is able to intervene in human and natural affairs without the aid of an intermediary (such as a priest, medicine man, or ancestors). As a numinous (spiritual) being, he is closer to man than other spiritual powers. He sends lightning and rain and rules the stars that are, at most, essential aspects of himself or are members of his family subject to him. He is the creator and the receiver of the dead. Modern scholars have designated such a being as the "high god," "supreme god," the "highest being" of the "original monotheism," the idealized god of heaven, or the familiar father deity. Very human, often comical, or even unethical and repulsive traits of such deities are often represented in myths that also sometimes include legends of animal or human ancestors.

The withdrawn god. The god of heaven may be a Deus otiosus, who has, after completing the creation, withdrawn into heaven and abandoned the government of the world to the ancestors of men or to nature spirits that are dependent on him and act as mediators between him and men. This type of god, who is able to intervene directly only when there are widespread existential necessities or needs (such as drought, pestilence, or war), can be found primarily where worship of the dead or worship of individual local "earth spirits"—not yet integrated into an all-inclusive earth deity—obscures everything else.

The first among equals. The god of heaven also may be the head of a pantheon of gods, the first among equals, or the absolute ruler in a hierarchy of gods. This occurs in polytheism (belief in many gods) in its purest form. The deities associated with him are often related to him by family ties (genealogies of gods). Occasionally, the heavenly phenomena are distributed among members of the clan of gods, the god of heaven himself thus becoming rather vague. The divine pair, heaven-earth, represents only one among many possible combinations, such as Dyaus-pitri (heaven, male) and Prthivi (earth, female) in Vedic India or, with an unusual distribution of the sexes, Nut (heaven, woman) and Geb (earth, man) in ancient Egypt.

ternatives—these ups and downs, for he or she wishes finally to be in a place where there is simply balance, beyond heaven and hell in a place of absolute freedom from all influences of desire and hope, and therefore imbalance.

In effect, Moksha is when bliss has become natural and permanent, and heaven and hell have merged as one truth. This third state is the aim of the Hindu, where there is no flickering back and forth like a candle in the wind—good, bad; happy, sad; excited, depressed. You are

Occasionally, generations of gods succeed each other (such as in Greece and western Asia). In such instances the more universal god of heaven is often replaced by the younger god of thunderstorms (Zeus of the Greeks, Teshub of the Hittites, or Hadad of the Semites) or is even relegated to the background by a goddess, such as Inanna-Ishtar (the love or fertility goddess in Babylonia) or Amaterasu (the sun goddess of Japan).

In ancient China, heaven (T'ien, or Shang Ti, the highest lord) ruled over the many more popular gods and was even closely related to the representatives of the Imperial household. Deification of the celestial emperor is a cultic practice that extends from Korea to Annam (part of Vietnam). The roots of the worship of heaven in Asia are probably the beliefs of central and northern Asiatic nomadic peoples in a solitary god of heaven. Gods of heaven, above or behind a pantheon (grouping of gods), probably originated in areas where a theocratic stratified bureaucracy existed or where sacral kingdoms exist or have existed.

free and blissful wherever you are and whatever you do once you attain Moksha. Moksha is to abandon the differences altogether. The following story is useful as an example of this.

There was a great Hindu saint who was never known to be sad. He was nearing 90, but he was always happy, cheerful, and bubbling with joy, like a small child. People gathered together one day to celebrate his ninetieth birthday. As this might be the saint's last birthday, all his disciples had come from faraway places. They asked him, "We have only

one question. Soon you may leave us—your body is getting older and
older. Before you leave, please answer: What is the secret of your joy?
Nobody has ever seen you sad."

The old man laughed. He said, "There is not much of a secret in it.
Early in my life I discovered that it is up to me to be in hell or to be in
heaven, so every morning when I wake up, the first thing I ask myself
is, 'What do you want today—heaven or hell?' And I always decide for
heaven! That is my simple secret."

In the Western religious mind this way of seeing good and evil is
often forgotten. The idea of achieving permanent bliss during this life
is beyond our normal understanding, for we have been taught that it is
not possible. We do not understand or believe that we have a choice.

So prayer in the Hindu tradition has never been a matter of desiring something that might or might not happen. For Moksha can only
be achieved through a determination for joy. Consciousness, though it
may seem to us to be an esoteric doctrine, is in fact simply another determination, achieved by practice.

There is another ancient Hindu story that tells of a man who came
to the Hindu heaven and found the equivalent of the Christian Tree of
Knowledge. This tree in the Hindu heaven is called Kalptaru, which
means the "wish-fulfilling tree." The man was exhausted from his travels and therefore sat down beneath the tree. As he sat he realized how
hungry he was, and immediately after he had the thought, food
appeared, so he ate it. Then he felt sleepy and thought of how nice it
would be if there were a bed for him to lie on. The bed appeared, so he
lay down on it, ready to sleep deeply. But as he lay there he began to
wonder how all this was happening. How could there be food and a
bed suddenly without anyone being there to provide them? He
became frightened and thought maybe that there were ghosts around
playing tricks on him. As he thought of the ghosts, they appeared before him and terrified him out of his wits. He became so frightened
that he feared they would kill him, so they did.

We, too, manufacture our own lives out of the prayers we make,
for our prayers are projected into existence, into life, and make our joy,
misery, complications, desires, pleasures, failures, and successes. If we

can manage to see heaven and hell as one truth rather than two alternatives, then we manufacture our prayers and our lives from that understanding.

This was the foundation of mysticism in the very early years of Christianity as much as it was in Hinduism. Truly, heaven is allowing oneself to live joyously, hell is preventing it, and purgatory is insulating ourselves from both. It all flows together as one and depends for its negative existence only on our personal sense of separation and division.

The most ancient traditions understood prayer as arising from a form of complete silence that emanated from the very being of the individual, creating no desires, no thoughts at all, but a simple silent space into which life could pour continuously. Praying from this undivided being in a state of silence produces only bliss, and in this bliss all desires are fulfilled automatically. This is possible for everyone, Western or Eastern, Jewish, Christian, Hindu, Mohammedan, Buddhist, even agnostic or atheist.

BUDDHA'S ROSE

HE CONCEPT OF PRAYER AS ARISING OUT OF SILENCE AND peace was also given credence by the extraordinary presence of Gautama the Buddha. It is worth telling the story that gives us the best feeling for how Buddhism was born as a study of the divine from a perspective of silence. Strictly speaking, this was the beginning of Zen Buddhism.

One morning when Buddha arrived to speak before his disciples, he came carrying a flower. This was not a normal thing for him to do, for as a habit, he would come empty-handed.

He sat in his normal place, beneath his favorite tree, and remained completely silent, gazing at the flower. He said nothing and looked at no one, only gazing at the flower continuously. This went on for more than an hour, until the disciples sitting before him became restless and uncomfortable. Nevertheless, Buddha did not move or make any sound.

The story tells that one disciple, named Mahakashyapa, burst into laughter, and Buddha summoned him to sit before him and handed the flower to him. He told Mahakashyapa and the disciples that he had given them all that could be given in words, and that which could not be given in words he was now giving to Mahakashyapa. This final idea was the key to everything, and it could not be communicated verbally.

This story gives rise to what the Buddhists call "transferring the key without scripture." The "information" is beyond writing down, beyond speaking, and beyond the mind. It is a mystical experience that can only be shared as an experience of the heart and soul. Mahakashyapa thus became the first holder of the key, which was handed down to the succeeding Zen patriarchs, until it reached Bodhidharma, who left India and went to China, where Zen (known there as Ch'an) first came, and subsequently spread to Japan and other countries.

Gautama the Buddha (circa 550 B.C.E.) was founder of Buddhist and Zen Buddhist religious understanding and a unique mystic. He had a unique reputation as a superb teacher. His conversion and taming of Angulimala, a murderer and bandit who was a terror even to Pasenadi, the king of Kosala, is put forward as an example of his great powers and abilities. People who went to see and hear him were fascinated and were so quickly converted to his new teaching that his opponents described him as having some enticing trick. King Pasenadi is reported to have said that those who went with the idea of confounding Buddha in debate became his disciples at the end. Full of compassion and wisdom, he is recognized as knowing how and what to teach individuals for their own benefit according to the level of their capabilities.

Buddha refused to recognize the religious significance of the caste system that was a long-established and respected institution in India and recognized the religious potential of men and women of all social ranks. He also recognized the connection between economic welfare and moral development. Trying to suppress crime through punishment, he said, was futile. Poverty, according to Buddha, was a cause of immorality and crime; therefore, the economic condition of people should be improved.

To those who understand the art of silence, this story is the whole "scripture" of Zen Buddhism. In fact, it could be said to be the whole story of all religion, as it epitomizes the understanding of transference—communication through silence.

THE TAO—PRAYING
THROUGH HARMONY
છ

NE OF THE OTHER MOST PROFOUND EASTERN FORMATIONS of prayer arises from perhaps the subtlest of all religious foundations: Taoism (pronounced "dowism").

The school of Taoism began some time around 100 B.C.E. with the identification by its early proponents of three masters: Lao-tzu, Lieh Tzu, and Chuang Tzu. The title "Tzu" is an honorific one and means, literally, "master." The strange but nevertheless appropriate aspect of Taoism is that all three of these masters are veiled in a kind of mystery, two of them more so than the third. Lao-tzu and Lieh Tzu are both almost impossible to trace as having actually existed. There is no strictly definable source for their lives anywhere, and even the famous book *Tao Te Ching*, which was supposed to have been written by Lao-tzu, probably wasn't at all. It was more than likely a compilation put together by several people whom we do not know anything about either.

Though this may sound somewhat bizarre, it is actually appropriate, for the basis of Taoism is a kind of nonexistence. The most fundamental tenet of the belief is encapsulated in the phrase taken from *Tao Te Ching*: "The Tao that can be told of is not the eternal (true) Tao."

Again we find the same concept echoed as with the ancient mystical Eastern and Western scriptures (such as the Celtic faiths or Vedism). If it is uttered, either written down or spoken, it is not real, and it is not the Tao. The two greatest masters of Taoism, therefore, are veiled in mystery, as though they lived only as a kind of unspoken myth. The third master—Chuang Tzu—does appear to have some reality, though even here the only records of his life emerge from the first great historian of China, Ssu Ma Chien, who lived in China toward the end of the years before the Christian era began and wrote a book called *The Book of Chuang Tzu*, which outlined all the Taoist teachings of Lao-tzu and Lieh Tzu, whom he names as the founders of Taoism. This book and *Tao Te Ching* are accepted today as the basis for Taoism, and their fundamental understanding of religiousness and life, of God in the ultimate sense, is that the act of prayer, or contact with life's God, is best effected in a state of harmony with nature (in the sense of existence). It is worth giving the whole of the quote from *Tao Te Ching*. This is a truly Taoist prayer.

> *The Tao that can be told of is not the eternal Tao;*
> *The name that can be named is not the eternal name.*
> *The Nameless is the origin of Heaven and Earth;*
> *The Named is the mother of all things.*
> *Therefore let there always be nonbeing, so we may see their subtlety,*
> *And let there always be being, so we may see their outcome.*
> *The two are the same,*
> *But after they are produced, they have different names.*
> *They both may be called deep and profound*
> *Deeper and more profound,*
> *The door of all subtleties.*

Essentially, Taoist prayer arises from a state of what is known as nonbeing, which, put another way, is a state in which mental activity—thought—is of lesser importance than a profound harmony with life, all life that is, or what has also been described as "isness," or "itness."

This rather obscure and indefinable state is exactly that—indefinable—for it arises out of the being of the individual, where there is silence from the chattering of the mind. Many spiritual writers have given their best to come up with something verbal for this basic concept of life, but at best it comes through as poetic or inspiring.

One of the great American spiritual writers has a better way of describing this than most.

> *The spiritual is not to be separated from the material, nor the wonderful from the ordinary. We need, above all, to disentangle ourselves from habits of speech and thought which set the two apart,*

making it impossible for us to see that this—the immediate, every-day, and present experience—is IT, the entire and ultimate point of the existence of the universe.

ALAN WATTS, *THIS IS IT AND OTHER ESSAYS ON ZEN AND SPIRITUAL EXPERIENCE*

Essentially, this "itness" is life—the entire and ultimate point of existence. All the everyday bits and pieces that we inject into this life that we call our own are mere nothings, and of no significance, in the face of the miracle of IT. And IT, in this case, is the Tao.

MONASTICISM

❦

C HRISTIANITY HAS HAD ITS OWN VERY POWERFUL OFFERING to make in the realms of silence, contemplation, and prayer. The monastic tradition arose out of the need for sacred places for the inner life, contemplation (meditation), prayer, and a direct connection with God.

Monasticism is based on the Christian ideal of perfection and has its roots in New Testament Christianity, in which the baptized were designated as the "perfect ones." In the early Church monasticism equated perfection with world-denying asceticism, along with the view that perfect Christianity centered its way of life on the maximum love of God and the "neighbor."

Monastic discipline, in the course of time, became an external means for the attainment of this ideal of perfect love of God and neighbor. Only a few especially disciplined persons, however, have been able to live according to the Christian path that leads to the ideal of perfection. The monastic tradition was therefore not intended to be echoed in the everyday life of ordinary people, but the basis for it was seen as an example to be drawn from.

By the fourth century, monasticism had become an established institution in the Christian Church. Out of the desire for still further advanced isolation, ascetics moved from areas in proximity to inhabited places and established themselves in tombs, abandoned and half-deteriorated human settlements, caves, and finally, into the wilderness areas of the deserts. The main task of the ascetics—that is, struggle with the demons—thereby underwent a heightened intensification: The desert was considered the abode of the demons, the place of refuge of the pagan gods falling back before a victorious Christianity.

A former Roman soldier of the fourth century, Pachomius, created the first monastery in the modern sense. He united the monks under one roof in a community living under the leadership of an abbot (father, or leader). In 323 C.E. he founded the first true monastic cloister in Tabennisi, north of Thebes, in Egypt, and joined together houses of 30 to 40 monks, each with its own superior.

Western monasticism, founded by Benedict of Nursia (Italy) in the sixth century, has gone through a double form of special development vis-à-vis early church monasticism. The first consists of its clericalization. In modern Roman Catholic cloisters monks are, except for the serving brothers (fratres), ordained priests and are thereby drawn in a direct way into the ecclesiastical tasks of the Roman Church. Originally, however, monks were laymen.

The second special development in Roman Catholicism consists of the functional characteristics of its many orders. The individual orders aid the church in its various areas of activity—missions, education, care for the sick and needy, and combating heresy. Developing a wide-ranging diversification in its structure and sociological interests, Roman Catholic monasticism has extended all the way from the knightly orders to orders of mendicant friars, and it has included orders of feudal and aristocratic characteristics alongside orders of purely bourgeois characteristics. To the degree that special missionary, pedagogical, scholarly theological, and ecclesiastically political tasks of the orders increased in the West, the character of ancient monasticism—originally focused completely on prayer, meditation, and contemplation—receded more and more in importance. Few monastic orders—the Benedictines and the Carmelites are notable exceptions—still attempt to preserve the ancient character and purposes of monasticism in Roman Catholicism in the twentieth century.

The basic characteristic of monasticism was therefore to provide a profound example of the most extreme kind. The monk or nun was seen as an example of the ideal nature of prayer and contemplation through asceticism. The monk was not worldly in any way. He was in touch with the divine through the spoken prayer, and this prayer arose out of the deep practice of contemplation born out of a life of silence and unworldliness.

The fundamental difference between this Western tradition and the Eastern traditions that we have sampled was that Western prayer was directed through the spoken word of chanting and repetition, but this expression was nevertheless born out of a state of silence and remote peace. The individual monk or nun connected with God from a space of stillness. In this sense there is little difference between it and the meditation that was and still is undertaken by Hinduism and the other Eastern traditions. In the most profound Western tradition of prayer, the mystical connection of the unknowable was upheld.

SILENCE AS OUR BASIS FOR PRAYER

ॐ

*To bring the heart into tune with God is better
than audible prayer.*

MARINA DE GUEVARA

HE ANCIENT CELTIC TRIBES OF EUROPE, ONE OF THE OLDEST and most sophisticated of the old cultural heritages from our Western past, also believed in the concept of the unknowable and mystical. Their religious ceremonies (secret gatherings) were never recorded, but passed on to the next generation by the experience of being part of the ceremonies and rituals. To this day, we do not really know how the ancient Druids actually performed their rituals.

The Celts, Hindus, Buddhists, Jainas, Taoists, and many other religious cultures of the past shared their mystical experiences amongst their own people—those who understood—and for them, the very act of writing down or speaking was an act of loss.

The great pleasure and joy of this understanding of prayer is that it does not only come about through the handing of a flower to a friend or lover, but it can take any form. It can take the form of the Japanese Tea Ceremony, the Sufi dances and songs, the whirling Dervish movements, the African dances, the Song of Sahara, the movements of a tai chi master, ballet, the reading of a poem, even the cooking of a delicious meal, drinking a glass of wine, or making love. Eventually, all life becomes a continuous prayer to the divine. And in this state of continuous prayer we can choose Moksha as our way of life—we can choose to be in heaven even if life is hell for others. The moment-to-moment prayers out of our anxiety then transform into prayers out of clarity and joy.

Anything that is "spoken" from the heart can be a prayer to the divine, and so we have formulated our rituals and our beliefs in this way

Jainism. The Jaina's religious goal is the complete perfection and purification of the soul. This can occur only when the soul is in a state of eternal liberation from and nonattachment to corporeal bodies. Liberation of the soul is impeded by the accumulation of karmans, which are bits of material, generated by a person's actions, that bind themselves to the soul and consequently bind the soul to material bodies through many births. This has the effect of thwarting the full self-realization and freedom of the soul. To understand how the Jainas perceive and address this problem, it is first necessary to explain the Jaina conception of reality. Time, according to the Jainas, is eternal and formless. It is conceived as a wheel with 12 spokes called aras (ages), 6 making an ascending arc and 6 a descending one. In the ascending arc (utsarpini), man progresses in knowledge, age, stature, and happiness, while in the descending arc (avasarpini), he deteriorates. The two cycles joined together make one rotation of the wheel of time, which is called a kalpa.

The world is eternal and uncreated. Its constituent elements, the six substances (dravyas), are soul, matter, time, space, the principles of motion, and the arrest of motion. These are eternal and indestructible, but their conditions change constantly. Jainas divide the inhabited universe into five parts. The lower world (adholoka) is subdivided into seven tiers, each one darker and more tortuous than the one above it. The middle world (madhyaloka) consists of concentric continents separated by seas, the center continent of which is called Jambudvipa. Human beings occupy Jambudvipa, the second continent, and half of the third; the focus of Jaina activity, however, is Jambudvipa, the only continent on which it is possible for the soul to achieve liberation. The celestial world (urdhvaloka) consists of two categories of heaven: one for the souls of those who may or may not have entered the Jaina path and one for the souls of those who are far along on the path and are close to the time of their emancipation. At the apex of the occupied universe is the siddhashila, the crescent-shaped abode of liberated souls (siddhas).

down the ages. All the traditions and rituals of religion and life, both Eastern and Western, have grown from this silent space within humanity.

Jiddu Krishnamurti (1895–1986). One of the most important mystical teachers of the twentieth century, Krishnamurti was adopted by the Theosophical Society as the Messiah, a title that he eventually abandoned, dismantling the organization that had named him as such.

Krishnamurti's teaching was essentially mysticism without organized religion, and a direct synergy with nature and life as god. Traveling in India, America, and Europe (mostly Switzerland), he spoke to thousands of people on the subject of life as a portrayal of God, and the process of compassionate understanding. Meditation was the centerpiece of his understanding, that to settle into silence and stillness was an essential aspect of joy and beauty.

His personal life was involved in the presence of mystical beings whom he believed directed the world through their presence in the Himalayan mountains as a sort of subliminal presence that accommodated the reality that we observe in everyday life.

He lived into his nineties, giving discourses right to the end.

Bringing the heart in tune with God was seen by our ancestors as the essential aspect of prayer. This could and can be accomplished by finding that space of stillness and silence, whether through meditation, chant, ritual, or the spoken prayer. This gave rise to the building of places of worship, for here was an atmosphere, set aside especially for the task, where silence could more easily exist on the outside and therefore be emulated on the inside. Here is the source of both meditation and prayer.

So what has become essential in our present age is the encouragement of as much of that silent space as can be achieved—through prayer circles, prayer journals, prayer friends, even prayers on the Internet, right up through places of worship and the use of prayer to influence the way the world grows. The twentieth-century mystic J. Krishnamurti said that a hundred people in prayer, sitting together, can change the world.

THE TRADITIONS
OF PRAYER

COMMUNICATION WITH THE DIVINE WAS, FROM ITS beginning, undertaken from a human need, and so also were the terms that arise from it—terms like Father, King, Lord, Mother—whether these were used to address natural forces, such as a sun god; a benefactor of human activity, such as the goddess of health or childbirth; an ancestor; or the final creator, God himself. The same forms of speech have always been used, such as confession of sins, requests or thanks for help, and praise.

Perhaps the most primitive, but still today the most common, features of prayer are desires for freedom from earthly sickness and danger and the desire to gain earthly goods. Well-being is the essence of these original kinds of prayer.

These most ancient forms of prayer, found originally among preliterate peoples, lived on into civilizations where they developed from spontaneous, free expression into various formulas, such as hymns and psalms. Hymns became poetic contemplations on the nature of God's work and reached a high point in ancient Egypt, where they were sung to the Egyptian king Ikhnaton, for example. Some of these hymns and other prayers from ancient civilizations can be found beginning on page 76.

As religion developed into more complex formats, so prayer altered also. Requests for earthly goods very often ceased to occur altogether in the prayers of some cultures, particularly in Eastern countries such as India and China, where the spiritual aspect of religion has almost always been the most prevalent. Union with God, or godliness, was the most important characteristic of prayer. Many of the greatest and most important scriptures of each of the faiths can be seen as prayers themselves. The Upanishads are, in a very real sense, a long and extremely powerful prayer. The Bhagavad Gita, the basic scripture of

Saint Augustine (died circa 604 C.E.). He was the first archbishop of Canterbury and the apostle of England, who founded the Christian Church in southern England.

Probably of aristocratic birth, Augustine was prior of the Benedictine monastery of Saint Andrew, Rome, when Pope Saint Gregory I the Great chose him to lead an unprecedented mission of about 40 monks to England, which was then largely pagan. They left in June 596 C.E., but, arriving in southern Gaul, they were warned of the perils awaiting them and sent Augustine back to Rome. There Gregory encouraged him with letters of recommendation and he set out once more. The entourage landed on the Isle of Thanet, off the southeast coast of England, and was well-received by King Aethelberht (Ethelbert) I of Kent, who gave the missionaries a dwelling place in Canterbury and the old Saint Martin's Church, where he allowed them to preach. With Aethelberht's support, their work led to many conversions, including that of the king. In the following autumn Augustine was consecrated bishop of the English. Thousands of Aethelberht's subjects were reportedly baptized by Augustine on Christmas Day 597 C.E., and he subsequently dispatched two of his monks to Rome with a report of this extraordinary event and a request for further help and advice. They returned in 601 C.E. with the pallium (symbol of metropolitan jurisdiction) from Gregory for Augustine and with more missionaries, including the celebrated Mellitus, Justus, and Paulinus.

Augustine founded Christ Church, Canterbury, as his cathedral. Canterbury Cathedral was made and remains today the seat of the archbishop and primate (highest ranking bishop) of the Anglican Communion.

The Upanishads ("Sittings Near a Teacher"). The Upanishads were the last component of the Vedas, the mystically oriented and originally esoteric texts of Vedism. Vedic ritualism and the doctrine of the interconnectedness of separate phenomena were superseded by a new emphasis on knowledge alone—primarily knowledge of the ultimate identity of all phenomena, which merely appeared to be separate. The phase of Indian religious life roughly between 700 and 500 B.C.E. was the period of the beginnings of philosophy and mysticism marked by the Upanishads. Historically, the most important of these are the two oldest, the Brhadaranyaka ("Great Forest Text") and the Chandogya (pertaining to the Chandogas, a class of priests who intone hymns at sacrifices), both of which are compilations that record the traditions of sages (rishis) of the period, notably Yajñavalkya, who was a pioneer of new religious ideas.

The primary motive of the Upanishads is a desire for mystical knowledge that would ensure freedom from "re-death." Throughout the later Vedic period, the idea that the world of heaven was not the end—and that even in heaven death was inevitable—had been growing. For Vedic thinkers the fear of the impermanence of religious merit and its loss in the hereafter, as well as the fear-provoking anticipation of the transience of any form of existence after death, culminating in the much-feared repeated death (punarmrtyu), assumed the character of an obsession. The means of escaping and conquering death and of attaining integral life devised in the Brahmanas were of a ritual nature, but in the Brhadaranyaka (from sometime between the tenth and fifth centuries B.C.E.), more emphasis was placed on the knowledge of the cosmic connection underlying ritual. When the doctrine of the identity of atman (the Self) and brahman was established in the Upanishads, the true knowledge of the Self and the realization of this identity were substituted (by those sages who were inclined to meditative thought) for the ritual method.

Hinduism, is a prayer to the power and the mystical beauty of godliness. Later, the Islamic Qur'an is regarded as a book of prayers, and the book of Psalms from the Bible is viewed as a meditation on biblical history turned into a poetic form of prayer. Even the Confessions of Saint Augustine (354–430 C.E.), the unique Christian philosopher and theologian, is in effect a very long and devoted prayer to God.

All are longings to enter into a relationship with the divine and very rarely form quantifiable desires for specific needs or fears for loss of life. They are passionate inscriptions of individuals and groups who have experienced mystical bliss and a connection with existence.

Their use may not always have been for true meditation and prayer, for this, of course, depends on the individual employed in the act of praying. Some would say that the use of such scriptures for personal manipulation and designed acquisition is the definition of magic, that making use of the mystical for private gain is the difference between the sacred and the profane. And thus we see the division that took place, particularly in medieval Europe, between mysticism and magic, between God and, ultimately, the devil. But this division is beginning to disintegrate today, as we discover the paths to the divine in a world that is concentrating on its religious heritage more than it has for many centuries.

THE DIVISIONS
OF PRAYER

E CAN LOOSELY DIVIDE PRAYER, FROM THE TIME OF THE existence of the early scriptures mentioned previously, into six forms. The choice of these categories is more psychological than historical.

Petition, which has become a word used to mean a kind of prayer in itself (metonymy), is the prayer form of request. However much we may wish to discourage the idea of asking existence for selfish needs, it is nevertheless something that we, as human beings, need to do. In the form of requests for good health, prosperity, long life, and success, the petition is probably the most common prayer in all major religions.

The Judeo-Christian-based religions (which include Islam) are perhaps the most determined of the major religions in the disapproval—though not a total censure—of prayer as manipulation, while other, more ancient religions have a greater tolerance. Hinduism, for example, which is based partly on the scripture called the Rig-Veda (believed by some theologists to be tens of thousands of years old), contains many prayers for very clear human desires.

Ultimately, as we have mentioned already, it is not that we should not wish for good things for ourselves through prayer—we are, after all, only part of an existence that loves us to be healthy, wealthy, and wise—it is more that we might find greater satisfaction in a prayer petition that comes from a silent space of longing. God as existence does not frown upon us and make moral judgments about how we kneel in prayer. God as existence, or life, is us, kneeling in prayer, so that all we are really doing is petitioning ourselves to treat ourselves well in the present and future. We, not some distant supernatural being, are the moral arbiters of our lives.

Confession is both an affirmation of the faith of the supplicant and an admission of human sin. We can trace this dual concept of faith and sin to some of the earliest sources. Zoroastrianism (one of the earlier formats of faith that contributed to Christianity) acknowledges the presence of faith as part of the renunciation of the devil. In still earlier primitive religions, believers understood that their sins would

Bhagavad Gita, the Indian religious poem from sometime between the first and second centuries C.E. is the earliest and finest exposition of the Bhagavata system. By the time of the Gita Vasudeva (Krishna), the hero of the Yadava clan was identified with the Vedic Lord Vishnu. Later, the deified sage Narayana, whose followers were originally called Pañcar atras, was assimilated, and, still later, the pastoral and amorous Krishna was added to the multiplicity of traditions.

The Bhagavatas believed in simple rites of worship and condemned Vedic sacrifices and penances. The sect may have been largely responsible for the spread of image worship among orthodox, upper-class Hindus. Few early Vaisnava images are still extant, but those that have survived are mainly from the Mathura area, perhaps the earliest being the image of Balarama, the half brother of Krishna, which is believed to be from between the second and first centuries B.C.E.

The Qur'an (Arabic: reading or recitation; often spelled "Koran"), the holy book of Islam, is regarded by believers as the true word of God as revealed to the prophet Muhammad. In its written form it is accepted as the earthly reproduction of an uncreated and eternal heavenly original, according to the general view referred to in the Qur'an itself as "the well-preserved tablet." The word *qur'an* is derived from the verb *qara'a*, "to read" or "to recite," but there is probably also some connection with Syriac qeryana, "reading," used for the scriptural lessons in the Syrian Church. In the Qur'an itself the word is not used with reference to the book as a whole but only as a term for separate revelations or for the divine revelation in general. The Qur'an is held in high esteem as the ultimate authority in all matters legal and religious and is generally regarded as infallible in all respects. Its Arabic language is thought to be unsurpassed in purity and beauty and to represent the highest ideal of style. To imitate the style of the Qur'an is a sacrilege within the Islamic faith.

The Vedas, meaning "Knowledge," is a collective term for the sacred scriptures of the Hindus. Since about the fifth century B.C.E., the Vedas has been considered to be the creation of neither human nor god; rather, it is regarded as the eternal Truth that was in ancient times directly revealed to or "heard" by gifted and inspired seers (rishis) who transcribed it into the most perfect human language, Sanskrit. Although most of the religion of the Vedic texts, which revolves around rituals of fire sacrifice, has been eclipsed by Hindu doctrines and practices, the absolute authority and sacredness of the Vedas remain a central tenet of virtually all Hindu sects and traditions. Even today, as it has been for several millennia, parts of the Vedas are memorized and recited as a religious act of great merit.

anger the gods and made sacrifices to tip the balance again. Even the Rig-Veda, as always more generous than other scriptures, acknowledges that Varuna is merciful even to him who has committed sin.

But the sin must always be connected to the willingness of the sinner to adhere once again to the faith he professes. Sin with only guilt isn't enough. Confession as prayer is the first step toward salvation, at least within Judaism and Christianity, while in Buddhism, monks confess monthly in public, without the benefit of privacy. This is prayer direct to God, and originates from the concept of self-discovery. If you know your darkest side, you begin to know yourself. In that sense we can also see confession as a form of psychoanalysis. The individual prays to himself—to the God within him—employing the clergy as sounding board or mirror.

Intercession is prayer for others. It occurred commonly in ancient and primitive religions, especially from the East, where the family, friends, and members of the village or tribe were mentioned in the prayers. It appears in ancient Greece, Babylon, and Assyria, with special priesthoods for intercession alone. We could also say that Christ-

Zoroastrianism is the ancient pre-Islamic religion of Iran that survives there in isolated areas and more prosperously in India, where the descendants of Zoroastrian Iranian (Persian) immigrants are known as Parsis, or Parsees.

Founded by the Iranian prophet and reformer Zoroaster in the sixth century B.C.E., this religion, containing both monotheistic and dualistic features, influenced the other major Western religions—Judaism, Christianity, and Islam.

ian saints are intercessors, and in Islam the Dervishes, who were believed to have particular powers, were considered responsible for the protection of groups by intercession. Finally, the best known intercessor is probably Jesus. When on the cross he prayed: "Father, forgive them, for they know not what they do." Intercession prayer is regarded as perhaps the most unselfish of prayer, the ultimate compassion for a people or a world.

Hymns are a form of praise prayer. Throughout all religions, and most commonly in the East, praise is a prayer for God, for the great universe, the power of existence, and the environment of Mother Earth. We praise that which is, in our view, vastly greater than we are ourselves. The whole festival of Thanksgiving is a festival of praise. The Qur'an contains large sections that are simply praise for the Creator.

Praise could be seen as a kind of pantheism, which beholds the divine in everything, and thus plays a predominant role in Eastern religions.

Adoration is a kind of totality of prayer, a complete reverence of the entire being of the one who prays before his God, as in the following Western passage: "Oh God, you are my Lord, you are my mother, you are father, the Lord of the mountains and valleys."

When the Pope arrives on new land, he falls to the ground and kisses the earth. This is a prayer of adoration. Isaiah's vision of the angels in the Old Testament is accompanied by a prayer of adoration: "Holy, holy, holy is the Lord of hosts; the whole earth is full of his glory."

In addition, there is a form of adoration that is practiced by Eastern religions in the most ancient past and right up to today among many of the modern religious sects, such as those propounded by J. Krishnamurti, Osho, Ramana Maharshi, Muktananda, Da Free John (Adi Da), and others—the adoration and connection with existence of

Osho (1931–1990), previously called Bhagwan Shree Rajneesh and Acharya Rajneesh, originally named Chandra Mohan Jain, was an Indian spiritual leader who preached an eclectic and yet somehow unique doctrine of Eastern mysticism, individual devotion, and sexual freedom.

He taught philosophy at Jabalpur University, where in 1955 he received his B.A. degree; he also attended the University of Saugar. He acquired the Rajneesh and took the honorific title Bhagwan (Hindi: "god"). After lecturing throughout India, he established an ashram (spiritual community) in Pune (Poona). By the early 1970s his charismatic style and his emphasis on spiritual freedom and sexual experimentation had attracted 200,000 devotees, many from Europe and the United States.

In 1981 Osho's disciples purchased a dilapidated ranch in Oregon, which became the site of Rajneeshpuram, a community of several thousand disciples. Osho was widely criticized by outsiders for his private security force and his ostentatious display of wealth, though this may be seen as largely a device to enrage Western society into looking at his teachings. By 1985 many of his most trusted aides turned out to be operating their own private agenda, and at Osho's demand they abandoned the movement, which was, because of their behavior, under investigation for multiple felonies, including arson, attempted murder, drug smuggling, and voter fraud in the nearby town of Antelope. In 1985 Osho was deported from the United States. He was refused entry by 21 countries before returning to Pune, where his ashram soon grew to thousands of members. In later years he adjusted his teaching somewhat on unrestricted sexual activity because of his predictions that AIDS would become a major world disease. Osho may be seen as perhaps one of the most significant, albeit misunderstood, religious teachers of this century.

silence. And here we return to our discussion of the mystics of old and their belief in the esoteric mysteries of life as god. The silent, mystical prayer of adoration is the prayer that comes from the heart and being of the individual and of groups of people. We can also call this meditation, for within the final connection with life as god there is no mind and no sound. There is only absolute stillness and the immeasurable mystery of godliness.

"I am God." These words have been spoken by many mystics in moments of extreme ecstatic prayer, where the individual merges in a

 **Ramana Maharshi** (1879–1950), also known as Venkataraman, was one of the great mystics of India, a Hindu philosopher, and yogi called Great Master, Bhagavan (the Lord), and the Sage of Arunachala, whose position on monism (the identity of the individual soul and the creator of souls) and maya (illusion) parallels that of Shankara (circa 700–750 C.E.). His original contribution to yogic philosophy is the technique of vicara (self-pondering inquiry).

Born to a middle-class, southern Indian, Brahman family, Venkataraman read mystical and devotional literature, particularly the lives of South Indian Shaiva saints and the life of Kabir, the medieval mystical poet. He was captivated by legends of the local pilgrimage place, Mount Arunachala, from which the god Shiva was supposed to have arisen in a spiral of fire at the creation of the world.

At the age of 17 Venkataraman had a spiritual experience from which he derived his vicara technique: He suddenly felt a great fear of death and, lying very still, imagined his body becoming a stiff, cold corpse. Following a traditional "not this, not that" (neti-neti) practice, he began self-inquiry, asking, "Who am I?" and answering, "Not the body, because it is decaying; not the mind, because the brain will decay with the body; not the personality, nor the emotions, for these also will vanish with death." His intense desire to know the answer brought him into a state of consciousness beyond the mind, a state of bliss that Hindu philosophy calls samadhi. He immediately renounced his possessions, shaved his head, and fled from his village to Mount Arunachala to become a hermit and one of India's youngest gurus.

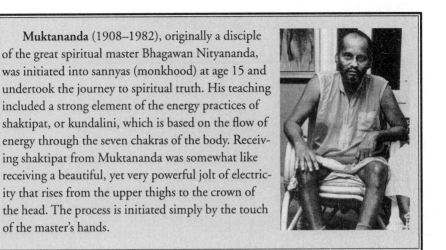

Muktananda (1908–1982), originally a disciple of the great spiritual master Bhagawan Nityananda, was initiated into sannyas (monkhood) at age 15 and undertook the journey to spiritual truth. His teaching included a strong element of the energy practices of shaktipat, or kundalini, which is based on the flow of energy through the seven chakras of the body. Receiving shaktipat from Muktananda was somewhat like receiving a beautiful, yet very powerful jolt of electricity that rises from the upper thighs to the crown of the head. The process is initiated simply by the touch of the master's hands.

union with the divine. There is no longer any separation from God or the gods, but a complete totality of perfect union. This is beyond ordinary experience. In fact, it is not experience at all, but a form of enlightenment.

Enlightenment is what we might call involuntary prayer, the individual becomes a mystic and cannot utter any words adequate to the experience. *Satori* is the word used by Zen Buddhists to describe an experience where nothing remains of the personality or character and all superficial fears and concerns of life vanish in the face of the vast divine. For Zen adepts, or highly skilled practitioners, it is a moment of complete explosion of the being into light and is accompanied with a full comprehension of life in all detail and simplicity—a sense of knowing everything, and that everything fits perfectly into a scheme that is comprehended perfectly without any need for mental explanation.

We find descriptions of this form of prayer in much modern written material, very often expressed with great poetry and beauty.

It was a morning in early summer. A silver haze shimmered and trembled over the lime trees. The air was laden with their fragrance. The temperature was like a caress. I remember—I need not recall— that I climbed up a tree and felt suddenly immersed in "Itness." I did not call it that name. I had no need for words. It and I were one.

BERNARD BERENSON, *SKETCH FOR A SELF PORTRAIT*

Da Free John (contemporary), lately known as Adi Da, was born Franklin Albert Jones on Long Island in 1939. It is claimed that he was born enlightened, and by the 1960s he began experiencing psychic phenomena. While staying in the ashram of Swami Muktananda he reached higher states of spiritual awakening and is said to have seen an apparition of the Virgin Mary. He then assumed the name of Bubba Free John and then Da Free John and Love Ananda, each name celebrating new stages of his rise to full enlightenment. He lives on an island in Fiji with close friends and devotees.

But here I had it, and sat like a bird on her nest, secure, unseen,
part of the distance, with the world, day and night, wind and light,
revolving round me in the sky. The distant and the near had no
longer any difference between them, and I was in the whole, as far
as my eyes could see, right to the sunset. The wind and the rain were
like the boiling elements in a glass flask, that was the entire earth
and sky held in my childish solipsist mind. The sun, the stratus
clouds, the prevailing wind, the rustle of dry sedge, the western sky,
were at one. Until the cold evening, or the rain, or the fear of the
dark drove me to run home for safety to the less perfect, the human
world, that I would enter, blinking as I came back into the light of
the paraffin lamp in the kitchen.

KATHLEEN RAINE, *FAREWELL HAPPY FIELDS*

Such is the reciprocity of human and divine in these events that god becomes the identity of he or she who prays. There is no religion that does not contain elements of this ecstatic form of prayer.

THE FORMS
OF PRAYER

෬

HE DIFFERENT KINDS OF WHAT WE CAN CALL FORMAL PRAYER throughout the world's traditions have fallen into fairly fixed patterns. They include: benedictions or blessings; litanies, which are petitions or responses to deities; ritual prayers; free prayers; formula prayers; hymns; and doxologies (prayers of praise). We find these throughout the very primitive ancient, Western, and Eastern forms.

From the very earliest sources, prayer was a connection with existence and the divine. In the most primitive, nonliterate tribes of today, the formats of prayer have remained much the same from their beginnings.

The primitive is dependent on his tribe and his god, or Supreme Being. He will express his prayers to various forms of this Supreme Being—the dead, nature, protectors, heaven, or Mother Earth. "Have pity on us"; "Bring rain for our crops"; "May our forefathers protect us"; and so on.

Internalized prayer is practiced by the Inuit of North America, the Semangs of the Andaman Islands, and the Australian Aborigines. It is an equivalent to meditation—a prayer in silence.

Other tribes, such as the Negritos of the Philippines, practice prayers in gestures and spontaneous prayers without any formal process.

Primitive prayer is essentially practical, concerned with personal well-being, protection of crops and food, and hopes for old age, but there are many tribes today, especially among the Australian Aboriginal tribes, where prayer is more developed. They have prayers for the dead so they can be well-received in heaven and prayers to the spirits accompanied by sacrifice. Some Aboriginal tribes also believe that excessive prayer, or prayer as simply a habit, serves no purpose.

The Inuit. The origins of the Inuit living in the western Arctic territories, largely in the coastal areas, are obscure. They constitute about one-third of the territorial population. Although several dialect groups are represented, all apparently have descended from what is known as the Thule culture, a

prehistoric maritime society. Early contacts with explorers and whaling crews introduced new diseases and reduced the population during the nineteenth century. There was also considerable interbreeding. The fur trade was not well-established in the Arctic until early in the twentieth century, but the Inuit adapted quickly to it, and they, like the Indians, came to depend upon outside sources of supply for most of the necessities of life. Construction activity during World War II and in the postwar years further affected their way of life. Inuit adapted readily to the opportunities for casual employment, and many were quick to abandon the seminomadic trapping and hunting existence for life in the settlements. Canadian government policy in the 1950s and 1960s promoted this trend in the interests of upgrading the quality of life.

Australian Aborigines. The archaeology of Australia shows that the continent has been occupied for at least 40,000 years; some scholars suggest that human occupation may date back 60,000 years. The Aborigines, whether in one or several periods, probably arrived either by way of the now submerged Sahul Shelf or, where land connections were absent, by rafts and canoes.

The tribes of the Australian Aborigines are unique, with a religious heritage based on dreams and an inner psychology in some ways far more complex than most Western civilized cultures.

Among ancient civilizations from about the third millennium B.C.E. to the beginning of the Christian period, prayer was a fairly constant practice among Assyrian and Babylonian cultures. The very earliest forms were litanies and hymns to the moon goddess Sin and the god Tammuz. One such is a hymn to Marduk, the Babylonian sun god, from the twelfth century B.C.E. and from a prayer kept in the library of Ashurbanipal, who was an Assyrian king during the seventh century B.C.E. At Ninevah there is a section of a long prayer to the goddess Nana, who was queen of the world and giver of life.

Prayers from ancient Egypt were inscribed on the back of scarabs in praise of divinities with statements of confidence and requests for protection for the one who prayed and his family: "God is the protector of my life; the house of one favored by God fears nothing."

There are also many Egyptian hymns of thanksgiving for illness and disease cured by the gods as well as much magical incantation using formulas, amulets, and charms. Some of these are attributed to magicians of the time and others to the gods themselves. *The Egyptian Book of the Dead* is a compilation of prayers for the dead that were composed, over a long period of time, to provide a smooth passage to the afterworld.

In ancient Greece prayers were poetic and ceremonial. Poetic prayers were composed of invocations to the gods followed by a justification for favors granted by the gods and a conclusion that outlines the request of the prayer. An example of this appears in the *Iliad*, written by the Greek poet Homer in the eighth century B.C.E.

Ceremonial prayers were ritualistic, accompanied by the washing of hands and the giving of sacrifice. One of the oldest preserved prayers comes from female devotees of Dionysus, who was the god of wine and fertility. This and other prayers to this god were largely erotic in nature, with hymns to the genitals and various exotic rites for the festivals of Bacchus.

Prayers from the Roman civilization had to be carefully addressed to the right god or goddess, as failure to make the correct address was believed to lead to potential disaster. There are litanies of 15 gods and goddesses, and the prayers take either the form of request or praise. Prayers of request were essentially, once again, very practical, seen literally as bargains with the gods. Temples were built in honor of the god or goddess, and in the extreme, the chief of the tribe offered to sacrifice himself in order to obtain victory. This was presumably why the correct address to the correct god was so important. To offer a "deal" to a god who was of no use in a particular circumstance would not help achieve the result. Prayer was a hard-and-fast business in ancient Rome.

Dionysus, also called Bacchus, or (in Rome) Liber, in Greco-Roman religion was a nature god of fruitfulness and vegetation, especially known as a god of wine and ecstasy. Though introduced from Thrace and Phrygia, the strange legends of his birth and death and his marriage to Ariadne, in origin a Cretan goddess, suggest that his cult represented a reversion to pre-Hellenic Minoan nature religion.

According to the most popular tradition, Dionysus was the son of Zeus and Semele, a daughter of Cadmus, king of Thebes, but in origin a Phrygian earth goddess. Hera, the wife of Zeus, out of jealousy persuaded Semele to prove her lover's divinity by requesting him to appear in his real person. Zeus complied, but his power was too great for the mortal Semele, who was blasted with thunderbolts. Zeus, however, saved his son by sewing him up in his thigh, keeping him there until he reached maturity, so that he was twice born. Dionysus was then conveyed by the god Hermes to be brought up by the Bacchants (Maenads, or Thyiads) of Nysa, a purely imaginary spot.

Within Western civilizations Judaism probably has the best known collection of prayers, the 150 Psalms within the Old Testament of the Bible. The Psalms are believed to have been composed over a period of some 500 years, dating back to the ninth and tenth centuries B.C.E. Their order and content were fixed for us today in the second century B.C.E. by the Septuagint, which was the translation of the Bible into Greek. This brought together, not always very expertly, four previous collections into one. The splicing kept the Psalms in order of their historical dating, and the first ones are clearly less sophisticated than the latter ones. To this extent they are not so very different in their intentions from any of the ancient prayers we've mentioned. They contain cries to God, confessions of sins, protestations of innocence, and imprecations against enemies.

To these prayers the Jewish rabbis added the Shema (Hear), which is a confession made up of three quotes from the Bible (Deuteronomy

6:4–9 and 11:13–21 and Numbers 15:37–41), which the people of Israel recite every day. At around the time of Jesus came the tefilla, or amida (standing prayer), which orthodox Israelis recite two or three times daily. In addition, there is the benediction before eating that raises the meal to a religious act.

Christianity has retained most of its Judaic inheritance and has added the Lord's Prayer, Psalms, canticles, hymns, and Christian prayer, which includes liturgical and personal prayer.

The liturgical collection includes readings from the Bible, collects, and a litany (a general prayer) for the intentions of the Church as a whole. During the Eucharist (Lord's Supper) there is a consecration of the bread and wine to be used during the sacred meal. The prayer is called the Eucharistic (Thanksgiving) Prayer. Originally spontaneous and improvised, it eventually became fixed into stereotyped formats, first in Western civilization and then, with more variations, in Eastern Christian areas.

In early Christianity, adherents kept the custom of praying three times a day, reciting the Lord's Prayer as well as giving a prayer at meals (a Jewish tradition, and one that was kept by Jesus himself). The original concept behind this day of prayer takes us back to the very source of religiousness—that life is a constant celebration of the divine.

For Islam, the most important prayer is the salat (daily prayer). The adept recites the prayer five times daily, with his body turned toward Mecca (in Saudi Arabia). Every Friday the salat al-jum'ah (Friday Prayer) replaces the prayer at noon. This is undertaken within the mosque with the whole local community. Twice annually, at the end of Ramadan and the tenth month, a solemn salat is celebrated.

All Islamic prayer is in adoration of Allah (God), and therefore no requests are included, as this is considered unworthy. The adept must clean himself with either water or sand before each prayer, prostrate his body, and be totally available to his god. The ultimate height of mysticism in Islam is known as Sufism.

To the Sufis, who in some senses are the high priests of Islam, prayer is very simple—it is a dance, a song, a complete celebration of

Sufism, also spelled *Sufiism*, is the mystic Islamic belief and practice in which Muslims seek to find the truth of divine love and knowledge through direct personal experience with God. Sufism consists of a variety of mystical paths that are designed to ascertain the nature of man and of God and to facilitate the experience of the presence of divine love and wisdom in the world.

The Arabic term *sufi* ("mystic") derives from *sufi*, "wool," probably in reference to the woolen garments worn by early Islamic ascetics. Sufism as an organized movement arose among pious Muslims as a reaction against the worldliness of the early Umayyad period (661 to 750 C.E.). Yearning for a personal union with God, the mystics found the externalities of the law, divorced from a personal theology, very unsatisfactory and increasingly asserted a way (tariqah, "path") and a goal (haqiqah, "reality") alternative to those of the Shari'ah, or traditional law. Sufism similarly opposed its intuitionism (ma'rifah, "interior knowledge") to the rational deductions of formal theology.

The mainstream of the Sufis strove to remain within orthodoxy and declared that the observance of the Shari'ah was indispensable; indeed, from the early period they had attempted to develop a scheme of partly antithetical and partly complementary categories (annihilation and restoration, intoxication and sobriety) to achieve a synthesis of the external and the internal. But the opposition of these two aspects continued to be emphasized. During the late twelfth and early thirteenth centuries, under the influence of speculative mysticism, Ibn al-'Arabi produced a system that created a complete chasm between the law and Sufism. In societies, such as Islamic India, that had a strong pre-Islamic heritage of mysticism, this chasm became much wider. Sufism developed into dervish orders, which emphasized emotionalism and hypnotic and ecstatic states and remained influential into the twentieth century.

all that is divine and holy. The incredibly beautiful whirling dances of the Dervishes are an example of this understanding of life, and once more bring us back to the origins of mysticism—an event that cannot be recorded, only experienced.

In the Eastern religions prayer existed in the Vedas before any of the Western prayer traditions began. The Vedic scriptures are believed to have been compiled between 8000 B.C E. and 1000 B.C.E. and represent natural forces of pantheistic belief rather than the classical theistic beliefs of Western religions. These scriptures include the Rig-Veda, the Brahmanas, the Bhagavad Gita, and the Upanishads, and are probably the most ancient recorded religious doctrines in the world. The term *pantheistic* is the nearest we can get in the West to describe their content, for in fact they were written to represent the concepts surrounding the oneness of the universe, rather than simply the presence of God in everything. The following lines from the Mandukya Upanishad may help illustrate the tone of the Indian scriptures, which are often poetic in structure and deeply involved in an often successful attempt to express the final mysticism and mystery of life beyond the mind.

It is not outer awareness
It is not inner awareness
Nor is it suspension of awareness
It is not knowing
It is not unknowing
Nor is it knowingness itself
It can neither be seen nor understood
It cannot be given boundaries
It is ineffable and beyond thought
It is indefinable
It is known only through becoming it.

The fundamental idea is that prayer may be born from silence and the being of the individual and can often best be expressed through sharing mystical experience with another.

Within the Vedas there are private and liturgical prayers, hymns, morning and evening prayers—such as the savitu, which is a prayer for dusk—and finally, a benediction form of prayer.

Hinduism, which is a comprehensive title encompassing several different religions, grew out of the Vedas. Within these religions there

And lead us not into temptation,
But deliver us from evil.

Here is another version, also in popular use.

Our Father who art in heaven,
Hallowed be thy name;
Thy kingdom come;
Thy will be done
On earth as it is in heaven.
Give us this day our daily bread;
And forgive us our debts
As we have forgiven our debtors;
And lead us not into temptation,
But deliver us from evil.
For thine is the kingdom
And the power
And the glory
Forever.

The last four lines (known as the doxology) were probably added some time in the centuries following Jesus' death.

Even among Christian scholars there is much disagreement about the meaning and intent of this prayer. Some believe that it relates to man's existence on earth, though still that earth is somehow separated from heaven. Put another way, this view of the Lord's Prayer holds that Jesus intended to relate the words to everyday life—in terms of our need for food and sustenance, our need to eschew evil and temptation, and our need for and hope toward a better world that exists after life in heaven. Others consider it strictly eschatological, referring to the coming of the final apocalypse and the return of the Messiah (possibly at the end of this millennium). This is exemplified by words found in the Lord's Prayer.

Both these interpretations tend to place the individual in a position of powerlessness. The eschatological interpretation probably emphasizes this idea still further, because it also brings into play the

Lao-tzu (circa sixth century B.C.E.) was the first philosopher of Chinese Taoism and alleged author of *Tao Te Ching*, a primary Taoist writing. Modern scholars discount the possibility that *Tao Te Ching* was written by but one person, but readily acknowledge the influence of Taoism on the development of Buddhism. Lao-tzu is venerated as a philosopher by Confucianists and as a saint or god by some of

the common people and was worshiped as an Imperial ancestor during the T'ang dynasty 618 to 907 C.E.). Despite his historical importance, Lao-tzu remains an obscure figure. The principal source of information about his life is a biography in the Shih-chi ("Historical Records") by Ssu Ma Chien. This historian, who wrote in about 100 B.C.E., had little solid information concerning the philosopher. He says that Lao-tzu was a native of Ch'ü-jen, a village in the district of Hu in the state of Ch'u, which corresponds to the modern Lu-yi in the eastern part of Honan Province.

concept that until Jesus returns as the Messiah, we have no real responsibility to sort out our problems ourselves. One can be fairly sure that this is not what Jesus intended, for he was almost certainly no different in his understanding of life and the ideals he upheld from any of the other enlightened men and women of the past, such as Buddha, Mahavira, or Mohammed.

All these individuals taught that we each have full responsibility for our own actions and thereby our own world, and that that world is here and now on this planet, where heaven and hell exist side by side in our hearts and minds. The churches that grew out of the teachings of these individuals may have altered and adapted their words, but the basic message in each case is the same.

In addition, the prayer suffers from misinterpretations through translation. The Greek word *epiousion*, which has been translated as meaning "daily bread," has no known parallels in Greek writing and may even mean "for tomorrow." Put in this way, the line, "Give us this day our daily bread" could actually mean something completely different, such as "Give us a foretaste of the heavenly banquet to come."

Perhaps we can reinterpret the prayer as referring to a heaven that exists on earth.

What difference would this make to the way the lines read?

Our Father who lives on this heavenly Earth
Hallowed be your presence here and now,
Your earthly kingdom is come,
Your will is being done,
On this glorious earth.
Continue to give us sight, within our daily lives,
of the heavenly banquet,
And help us to forgive our blindness to it,
As we forgive others the same.
Help us to walk away from unconsciousness
And to be compassionate with evil
For this is the kingdom of heaven
For ever and ever, in the immortal soul.

What is most fascinating about the prayers that have been handed down to us over the ages of mankind is that they all basically say the same things. Our interpretation of them may vary according to how we have been conditioned and taught to use them, but if we set aside these beliefs, the message is invariably the same. It is suggested that if we base our prayers on an understanding and appreciation of joy on earth, the prayers may well be more useful to us and those that surround us.

From the most famous and habitual Christian prayer, we can move to a prayer that comes from a movie entitled *Babette's Feast*.

Oh, watch the day
Once again hurry off.
And the Sun bathe

Itself in the water.
The time for us to rest approaches
Oh God, who dwelleth in heavenly light.
Who reigns above in heaven's hall.
Be for us our infinite light
In the valley of the night.
The sand in our hourglass will soon run out.
The day is conquered by the night.
The glares of the world are ending,
So brief their day, so swift their flight.
God, let thy brightness ever shine.
Admit us to thy mercy divine.

The presence of God and heaven is apparent in the prayer, but the reflection of the divinity is grounded in earthly activities.

Within Judaism come similar sentiments.

Throughout all generations we will render thanks unto Thee
And declare Thy praise,
Evening, morning, and noon,
For our lives which are in Thy care,
For our souls which are in Thy keeping
For Thy miracles which we witness daily,
And for Thy wondrous deeds and blessings toward us at all times.
JEWISH SABBATH EVENING SERVICE IN PRAYERS FOR THE
PILGRIM FESTIVALS

Miracles are another subject that we tend to allocate to a divine presence more powerful than we are. If we look at the context of the miracle in this prayer, we realize that the miracles of the divine are around us all the time in everyday life—the miracle of the dawn, the flower, the sun shining on us and keeping us alive. These miracles happen every time we open our eyes.

I've read all the books but one
Only remains sacred: this

Volume of wanders, open
Always before my eyes.

KATHLEEN RAINE, *COLLECTED POEMS*

We also find prayers from the most ancient Eastern scriptures that have given birth to Hinduism and modern Indian religions, where we discover the same message spoken in different words.

He who consists of the mind, whose body is breath, whose form is the light of Consciousness, whose resolve is true, whose Self is space, containing all actions, containing all desires, containing all odors, containing all tastes, pervading this whole world, the unspeaking, the unconcerned; this my Self within the heart is smaller than a grain of rice, or a barley-corn, or a mustard-seed, or a grain of millet, or the kernel of a grain of millet; this my Self within the heart is larger than the earth, larger than the sky, larger than the heavens, larger than all these words.

THE UPANISHAD CHANDOGYA

Feel the extraordinary beauty and appreciation of godliness and earthliness that this ancient prayer offers. There is no need to aggrandize the god in heaven, for this god also exists on the very ground and in the very body we inhabit.

In Europe we find similar sentiments expressed within the ancient Celtic traditions. The Celtic otherworld was conceived of as a group of islands far across, or sometimes under, the Western ocean. Its eternally young inhabitants were believed to celebrate continuously with feasts, music, and warrior contests. Many heroes in the Irish sagas are lured away by women from these islands, and later Christian saints were said to have sailed off in search of them.

Based upon a fluid cosmology in which shape-shifting and magic bonds between humans and other creatures are commonplace, Celtic myths point to a strong belief in the transmigration of souls. Such artifacts as the Gundestrup Caldron (found in Denmark) and the so-called Paris relief depict scenes of shamanistic woodland ritual. Much of Celtic poetry well into the Christian period reflects a preoccupation

Mikhail Naimy (1889–1988) was born in the Lebanese village of Biskinta, a majestic and beautiful place, which is situated on the slope of Mount Sannin, overlooking the eastern Mediterranean, the site for his book, *The Book of Mirdad*. Educated in Palestine, Russia, and Washington, D.C., Naimy was a literary contemporary and friend of Kahlil Gibran and eight other young literati who founded a dynamic movement that revolutionized Arabic literature. He wrote 31 books, which were acclaimed as classics in the Arab-speaking world. He was one of the greatest spiritual writers of this century.

with transformations and animal consciousness. Trees were a central element in ritual, several types of wood being regarded as oracular. The letters of the alphabet and the names of the months were based on tree symbols. The Druids took their name from an ancient Indo-European word meaning "knowing the oak tree."

Irish cult life revolved around seasonal observances. One of the two greatest yearly festivals was Samain (November 1), Summer's-End or the Feast of the Dead. The other was Beltine (May 1); Bel's-Fire honored the god Belenus and his province of war, as well as other "goings forth" to pasture, to the hunt, to wooing. These periods were divided by the lesser feasts of Imbolc (February 1), the beginning of the spring season sacred to the goddess Brigid, and Lugnasad (August 1), the feast of the marriage of Lugus and the day of the harvest fair. Christianity attempted to absorb these great festivals, some of the original spirit of which can be seen in the corresponding modern observances. The attempts were almost wholly unsuccessful, as Christianity required, by that stage, a written dogma that left all true mysticism behind through its need to create rational ritual behavior.

Celtic religiousness, therefore, can be seen as an embodiment of the mystical in its purest form. Celtic mysticism, however, was subsumed into a position of paganism by our Roman Christian forefathers, though much has survived till today, at least in potential.

Here is a typical Celtic prayer, designed to welcome the spring equinox (March 21).

> *Glad harbinger of Light, welcome!*
> *Maiden of Grace, boy of laughter.*
> *Gifts of potency returning,*
> *Spring surprise, the rainbow's embrace,*
> *Quickening the heart with our breasts,*
> *Opened by our souls to grace,*
> *May the blessing remain,*
> *Welcome upon every face.*

And another prayer was invoked to entice the gods of Imbolc (the festival at the very beginning of spring, a time very often of icy climate) into the home.

> *Midwife of the mystical, open the door,*
> *Child of the infinite, enter in,*
> *Welcome the newborn truth,*
> *Welcome the spring beginning.*
> *You travel in cold and darkness,*
> *And arrive in warmth and light.*
> *May the blessed time of Imbolc*
> *Kindle all our souls,*
> *Returning a new birth to innocence and truth,*
> *From the lowest to the highest,*
> *In the heart of all beings that live.*

Many more prayers from all these cultures exist in the section of this book on the prayers themselves (see page 76).

Mankind has always seen prayer as of central importance to life and belief in the divine. Over the several thousand years that prayer has existed, it has neither progressed nor regressed, but has somehow remained constant and prevailing, almost like an organ of humanity. It has also given rise to thousands of great and enlightened masters, gurus, saints, sadhus, and priests, who cannot be categorized as necessarily either genius or simpleton, but of some special quality beyond description or judgment. Whether halting or mystical, ceremonial or personal, prayer has always expressed the experience of a mystery beyond the knowledge of mankind, as a dialogue or merging with God. It has also always risen out of the essential mysticism that cannot be named or described, its very essence being its unknowability.

HONORING THE DIVINE
IN EVERYDAY LIFE
ℰℐ

There is no prayer other than the awareness: "I am That."
SWAMI MUKTANANDA

IRACLES ARE NORMALLY APPORTIONED TO DIVINE PRESENCE.
Within the Christian Church, for example, a miracle can only
happen in very precise circumstances at the behest of one who
will eventually be canonized as a saint. Miracles can, within Christianity, of course, also be apportioned to God himself, or Jesus Christ.
Therefore, a heavy premium on the ability to make miracles lies only
with very few people. It is not accessible to ordinary humans like you
and me. This perfectly sound philosophy, which has existed in humanity for millennia, has its place, and contains some of the greatest mystical beauty that mankind has generated.

But the presence of such an appreciation of the miraculous, though
originally intended to make the heart flutter with the divine spirit and
make the eyes raise to the heavens, has sometimes tended to turn man's
eyes dull and reduced in spiritual vision. For if miracles only happen at
the hands of individuals we can never aspire to, how can we see the
miraculous with those same eyes, eyes that watch "ordinary" life pass
them by, seemingly without event? How can we appreciate the miracles that surround us every second? Not surprisingly, it is a form of
prayer that permits this sight to expand to the miraculous.

We can call prayer "Soul Language" and capitalize it to give it true
significance.

Soul Language includes every conceivable format of prayer: recitation, poetry, hymn, psalm, chant, meditation, love, longing, and
desire. It includes all forms of religiousness: belief in God in heaven,
pantheism, god and goddess worship, monotheism, atheism, agnosticism, and all else that makes mankind's heart beat for the universal di-

vine. So there is primarily no prejudice to Soul Language, no differentiation, judgment, war, or barrier whatsoever. Soul Language can appreciate the solemn and awesome beauty of the Christian God as well as Buddha and Allah. Essentially, therefore, by this definition, Soul Language is a universal language, and we all speak it. The ability to make miracles happen is also universal.

Just to inspire us, we can take two quotations from individuals who have understood the way.

When you sit contemplating your original nature, that is samadhi,
for indeed that original nature is your eternal mind. By samadhi,
you withdraw your minds from their surroundings, thereby making
them impervious to the eight winds, that is to say, impervious to

Samadhi ("total self-collectedness"), in Hindu and Buddhist religion and philosophy, is the highest state of spiritual awareness that an individual can achieve while still bound to the body and that unites him or her with the highest reality. Samadhi is a state of profound and utterly absorptive contemplation of the Absolute that is undisturbed by desire, anger, or any other ego-generated thought or emotion. It is a state of joyful calm, or even of rapture and beatitude, in which one maintains one's full mental alertness and acuity. Samadhi is regarded in Hinduism and Buddhism as the climax of all spiritual and intellectual activity. The power to attain samadhi is a precondition of attaining release from the cycle of rebirths (samsara). Hence, the death of a person having this power is also considered a samadhi. By a further extension, the site where a person believed to be so empowered was cremated is in modern times also referred to as a samadhi; thus, the site of Mohandas Gandhi's cremation in Delhi is officially named Gandhi's samadhi. A brief and essentially temporary glimpse of samadhi is known as satori, and can happen without warning to any individual in any situation without reason, even if that individual is in no way involved in any spiritual quest.

*gain and loss, calumny and eulogy, praise and blame, sorrow and
joy. By concentrating in this way, even ordinary people may enter
the state of Buddhahood.*

THE ZEN TEACHINGS OF HUI HAI

*And then our good Lord opened my ghostly eye, and showed me
my soul in the midst of my heart. I saw the soul so large as it
were an endless world, and also as it were a blessed kingdom.
And by the conditions that I saw therein, I understood that it is
a worshipful city.*

JULIANA OF NORWICH, *REVELATIONS OF DIVINE LOVE*

The "worshipful city" that Juliana of Norwich refers to is the heavenly world we live in, and the method of seeing it as miraculous is undertaken in Hui Hai's words: "When you sit contemplating your
original nature, that is samadhi, for indeed that original nature is your
eternal mind."

So how do we contemplate our "original nature"?

The "eternal mind" is something that includes the mind we use
every day, but it is a greater form of that mind, for it includes elements
of the human condition that are often not in use in our everyday lives.
The art of finding this eternal mind is achieved through the practice of
prayer. Try to allow prayer to arise from a space of silence within yourself, whether this prayer be verbal, spoken silently within the mind
and heart, or simply in a state of silent contemplation.

FINDING PRAYER WITHIN US

Whether He replies or not,
Keep calling Him—
Ever calling in the chamber
Of continuous prayer.
Whether He comes or not,
Believe He is ever approaching
Nearer to you
With each command of your heart's love.
Whether He answers or not,
Keep entreating Him.
Even if He makes no reply
In the way you expect,
Ever know that in some subtle way
He will respond.
In the darkness of your deepest prayers,
Know that with you He is playing
Hide-and-seek.
And in the midst of His dance of life, disease, and death,
If you keep calling Him,
Undepressed by His seeming silence,
You will receive His answer.

PARAMAHANSA YOGNANDA

 IND A PRIVATE, RELATIVELY QUIET SPACE AWAY FROM THE demands of life, away from normal family activities, work, and play. A quiet corner of a bedroom, study, or den will work well. This room should be, if possible, one in which we can close the door against intrusion. Here we can find our own space.

POSITION OF THE BODY. The way the body is positioned is important, not only to find the maximum space within us to allow contemplation but also to accommodate what we prefer aesthetically. We may sit, kneel, stand, or even lie down flat on our backs. Some may prefer to adopt the "lotus" position, which entails sitting in a cross-legged position with the back straight and the hands resting in the cup of the lap or on either side.

Take a plump cushion and place it according to the position you prefer. A sitting position can be aided by a wall or solid support for your back. If kneeling, you may wish to place the cushion facing a wall or "altar" or small makeshift "temple."

If you choose the sitting position, squat down either cross-legged or with your legs bent to one side or the other, or simply pushed out in front so your limbs are relaxed and you feel totally comfortable. The purpose of squatting cross-legged (if the body is sufficiently supple to do this) is that it creates a kind of circle of energy flowing up from the base of the spine, through the head, and down into the belly again. This is why meditation is sometimes called "contemplating the naval."

If you prefer to kneel in prayer, it is best to keep your back fairly erect, especially if you wish to hold a book between your hands in order to recite prayers. Alternatively, kneel close to a surface where the book can rest open.

CONDITION OF THE MIND AND FEELINGS. The art of prayer from silence is first to learn to allow whatever is happening to happen without comment. Prayer arising from our inner silence—the Soul Language—is not about deliberately attempting to stop the thoughts, for you will never succeed in doing this. The mind will simply comment on how quiet it is being. Thoughts will not stop just like that, particularly if you try to force them to. The more "will" that is applied, the more thoughts will occur.

So watch the thoughts going by, without comment, without attaching yourself to them. Maybe you are thinking about the bills you haven't paid, or the fact that you're late for an appointment, or that your mother was complaining about something that morning. Allow these thoughts to pass you by, like clouds in the sky. They will come

And the miracle is: If you can go into your suffering as a meditation, watching, to the deepest roots of it, just through watching, it disappears. You don't have to do anything more than watching. If you have found the authentic cause by your watching, the suffering will disappear...
OSHO, DISCOURSES

I asked the boy beneath the pines
He said, "The master's gone alone
Herb-picking somewhere on the mount,
Cloud-hidden, whereabouts unknown."
CHIA TAO, *MY COUNTRY AND MY PEOPLE*

Meditate in the morning and evening and at night before you go to bed. Sit quietly for about two minutes. You will find everything in your life falling into place and your prayers answered.
YOGASWAMI, *POSITIVE THOUGHTS*

again to remind you later; you need have no doubt about that. For the moment simply let them go. Only your identification with them will keep them recurring like a tape recording. If you simply accept their presence in your mind, they will disappear and be replaced by others in a constant stream of ideas and reminders. Allow them. No comment, no judgment, no follow-through, no problem.

The same applies to various things that will happen to your body. It will itch to remind you that it exists. It will twitch and ache, get hot or cold, fidget restlessly, and create problems with muscles and bones, fingers and toes. It is not accustomed to sitting in one place for a long time without activity, and it will let you know this. And the more you listen to it and respond to its "talking" to you, the more difficult it will be to find the Language of the Soul. Every diversion that the mind and body provide is an avoidance of this Language. Allow it to itch. Allow it to ache, allow it to grumble at your lack of attention. If you have managed to sit or kneel in an uncomfortable position, you are free to adjust it, but try not to fidget too much, for fidgeting makes more fidgeting.

Tell your body that you are here to find something that has remained hidden all your life (perhaps), and that it should rest and remain still for just awhile. Tell it this information gently and with compassion, not angrily, for the body deserves its habits, but will soon be content to stay still, if cajoled into doing so.

Listen to the feelings, the demands, the discomforts, and the songs of the body. Just listen without comment and allow them to be there.

The same also applies to the environment of the body—the sounds outside, like trees rustling in the wind, traffic noises outside the window, water running in the bathroom, distant TVs in other peoples' homes, creaking wood, ticking clocks. Let these sounds register in your senses, without comment, without desire to stop them or hush them. Allow.

Allow also the smells that drift across your nose. These will become more intense as you relax, for as the senses are given space without comment, so they increase in intensity. Your awareness becomes sharper. This is good. Allow it.

So everything is happening as normal, and your awareness, your consciousness—a purely practical gift that everyone possesses—continues while you begin to pray.

Finally, probably more powerful than all of the above, will come your emotions and moods. The prevalence of the human mind as a tool used by humanity during this century has arisen (among other reasons) because of our inability to accept our emotional makeup. We tend to be afraid of our feelings because they seem to be so powerful and unpredictable. We suppress them because they seem to dominate us. Anger leads to pain, fear leads to bad judgment, and desire leads to sorrow and disillusionment. So we sit on our feelings and hope they will go away. We deny them.

During your first few sessions of prayer, or Soul Language, these moods and feelings will surface more strongly than ever, for when you are silent and still, they get a chance to rise to the surface. The feelings will take advantage of the opportunity to let you know that they exist.

Emotions are also the most difficult to dis-identify with, as, having been suppressed for so long, they grab you by the throat and make you feel them more profoundly.

As with all the rest of the trappings of life, allow them to be there without comment. Let the guilt surface, allow the doubts to come up ("I'm no good at this. I'll never find the Language of the Soul. What chance have I got?") All this is fine. Just allow it to be there—no need to censor or congratulate yourself. Simply permit a lack of response to these habitual forms of human behavior. We all normally respond and then identify with the thought or feeling, but you, during this prayer exercise, are going to let it go by. In effect, what you are doing is giving yourself a rest from all this.

If you can watch any part of yourself behave, then this part is not really you. You can see your body, so you are not your body. You can see your mind, so you are not your mind. You can see your moods and feelings, so you are not these either. What you are is the watcher— pure awareness. It is from this place of awareness, this place of silence, that the Language of the Soul is spoken. From this sacred space you can pray in whatever way you wish, from any scripture preferred, from the prayers selected in this book.

This exercise of prayer should be done every day for perhaps 40 to 60 minutes, in silence, alone or with a close friend or friends. After a week or two you will begin to notice a new habit forming: the ability to watch the thoughts and feelings go by without comment. As you find yourself able to do this, so the rest of your life will change, for the incidence of worry and identification with fear and sadness will diminish. The constant chattering of the mind is nothing other than a habit like smoking or eating. It does not have to dominate you.

As it ceases to do so, so you will begin really to pray, every moment of every day. And as you pray, so the miracles will also start to happen. Events will begin to occur for you in the best ways you could possibly wish. You will begin to smell the flowers and see the sky, enjoy the miracles of everyday life on a constant basis. Effectively your eyes will open, perhaps for the first time in your life. Prayers will be answered, even though you may not have spoken a single word. The best things,

things that you could not possibly have expected, will occur. Even wealth, health, and happiness.

This is prayer in its purest form, and it applies to all religions without prejudice, all people without question, and all situations without discrimination.

There is no proposal here that this is the only way to pray. But there is a proposal that it is the basis for all prayer, whether it be in a Catholic church, an Islamic mosque, a Jewish synagogue, or a Hindu temple. There is no need, either, after a period of practice that such prayer takes place sitting or kneeling on a cushion on the floor. It may be undertaken kneeling before the Holy Cross, a statue of Buddha, or the image of Kali or visiting the local rabbi. It may eventually be undertaken sitting on a bus or train, working at a computer, attending a potentially stressful board meeting, or working in a factory. With this incredible tool we can pray at work or play, night or day, and in any part of the world, during any age of our lives.

We began this book by saying that originally, prayer was in constant use as a way of life that occupied every hour of every day:

> *In its earliest incarnations prayer was a way of life that occupied every hour of the day, not simply kneeling in prayer, but as a fabric of life, in thought, in deed, and in relationship with the world. Within the most ancient traditions, such as Vedism in India, which developed into the Hindu faiths, and within European pagan religions, such as those of the pre-Christian Celts, and Native Americans, prayer was a connection to existence in the broadest sense, a synergy with godliness, a part of mysticism.*

We might, at the time we first read this, have doubted the possibility that someone could pray all the time, but perhaps now, having looked more closely at the traditions and foundations, plus the practices of prayer out of silence, we can see how it could work, thus also drawing this part of the book into a circle, beginning and end.

THE POWER
OF PRAYER

❧

He whose joy is within, whose pleasure is within,
and whose light is within, that devotee, being well-established
in the Supreme, attains to absolute freedom.
THE BHAGAVAD GITA, *BOOK OF DAILY THOUGHTS*
AND PRAYERS

HE QUOTE AT THE BEGINNING OF THIS SECTION COMES
from the ancient Vedic scripture, which forms one of the
most profound bases for all prayer. Simply explained, it
tells us two things.

1. That the source of all life lies within us—that ultimately, there is
no other essential landscape than the inner landscape. The prayer that
arises out of a calm mind and heart is the beginning of that
understanding, and the Language of the Soul that we will learn by this
method provides the correspondence that we all need with the rest of
our world and the people that live in it. This is freedom, because we
cease to be blown about in the winds of change that extroversion
forces upon us. We accept and allow our thoughts, feelings, and
moods without permitting them to constantly alter our temperament.

2. That freedom in turn gives us choices. It empowers us to make
whatever choices we wish in life without fear and without anxiety,
greed, or suffering. There is no reason to live that we must somehow
grasp in order to be happy, rich, or successful. If this were not so, we
would all be searching for the same reason to live, and we are not, for
each of us has a different truth. Life is a blank slate—a white page—on
which we must write our own words. Opportunity for joy and
pleasure, success and love await us. We have only to find ourselves, and
then we can grasp whatever we choose. The reason for life exists within
us, simply in the knowledge of self, and this knowledge is found
through the Language of the Soul.

Once accepting of this basic truth, we may then begin to help others. It is at this time that our own personal and unique truth enables us to communicate, indeed, forces us to communicate, because with the inner light that we find, there has to be a shining outward.

PRAYER AT HOME. We have already looked at the way we pray, and this may be sufficient for some, but there are more elaborate and perhaps fun ways that we can equip our private "temples" with the surroundings that will enhance the pleasure of prayer.

Ideally, a space set aside for prayer will create harmonies, auras, and energy forms that bring us more easily into a silent state. The very first architects of churches and temples created them for this very reason— to attract silence and stillness into the place where people worship. Early European cultures within Celtic societies used tree arbors as their "churches" (which, incidentally, gave rise to many modern superstitions such as touching wood for good luck and avoiding crossing others on the stairs). Trees were planted in long lines with a suitable space between, in a kind of orchard arrangement. The Druids would use these arbors to pray in and conduct their religious rituals and mystical ceremonies.

We can just as easily create our own small temple within the home. The worshiper may wish to have a crucifix, a statue of Buddha or one of the ancient Hindu gods, or even the picture of a favorite guru or loved one as the centerpiece of the temple, placed on a special cloth with candles on each side. Good-smelling incense always helps evoke a religious sense in the mind and body. Many of the modern churches still use incense as an important part of their services, such as the extraordinarily beautiful religious rituals of Mass in the Roman Catholic Church.

Such an "altar" may be erected on a mantelpiece or windowsill, or on a bookshelf. Wherever the temple is created, there holiness is born and allowed to grow as it is used. There is nothing especially mystical about this; anyone can do it anywhere. The mysticism arises out of the intention and the attitude of the "disciple."

Times of prayer may be selected as regular moments of the day or night. We can choose these according to our practice—perhaps first thing in the morning, last thing at night, or both. The "temple" may also be used, of course, any time in between, and it will be noticed quite quickly just how kneeling or sitting before the private place of prayer aids moments of indecision or anxiety, and creates better actions out of previous dilemma. Prayer even increases creativity, as the creative spirit arises from a still being and is only spoiled by the complexity and anxiety of human fears and thoughts. We are, in essence, talking directly with God in these moments, and our prayers will be answered in every case, almost immediately, for this is the best form of "psychoanalysis," therapy, and the seeking of advice. The answers arise out of our own freedom and the unclouding of the mind and heart.

So our home temple becomes the very source of our joy and freedom, a place that we eventually love to visit each day and a place where we find what we need.

The home temple also reflects the inner beauty that we have and reflects it back at us—like a kind of mirror of the soul. Before it we speak the Language of the Soul, whether this be in silence, the uttering of a mantra, or the reciting of prayers.

PRAYER JOURNALS. A prayer journal is like a dream journal. Just as we get up in the morning and write down our dreams for better memory of them or to interpret them or use them as the basis for psychoanalysis, so we can do exactly the same with the results of our prayers. Buy or create a beautiful book as your prayer journal. Make it a special book that you write in with great care and precision. Record the prayers that you use or those that you have created. Who knows, you may need a particular prayer again sometime in the future. Record the results of the prayers—feelings, thoughts, events during the coming days—in your own life or the lives of others that you pray for. Keep the journal by or beneath your altar or temple so that it is enhanced by the holiness of your shrine. Keep a special pen to write with and leave this with the journal at all times so that you need not search for another one. Make everything imbued with the same elements of the divine, and your prayers will be all the more easily rewarded.

PRAYER CIRCLES. In the same way as you pray alone, you may also pray with others. You will find later in this book in "Locations for

Prayer" plenty of places where you can join existing prayer circles. They are scattered in almost every part of the world, some probably within reach of your hometown. And if there is nothing near enough for convenience, or if you prefer your own style and that of your local community or neighborhood, create your own prayer circle of friends. This can be done in your own home or someone else's or in a local hall or church. It can lead to all manner of other social contacts and bring great pleasure and good results to the groups that undertake it.

ELECTRONIC PRAYER. There are already an enormous number of prayer circles and centers on the Internet, examples of which are in the section, "Locations for Prayer." There are also literally hundreds of places on the Internet where anyone can ask for a prayer or send one to others. The beauty of the World Wide Web is that it connects millions of people who might otherwise never meet and allows them to share their most personal feelings and thoughts. Prayer on the Internet is a gathering of souls who are able and willing to speak the Language of the Soul.

PRAYER CHAINS. In the same way as there are chain letters for the desire to make easy money, so there are also prayer chains everywhere in the world, and it is simple to find them if you have an Internet connection. Some sources for these are in the section, "Locations for Prayer." You can also, of course, easily start one of your own, simply by writing a prayer and duplicating it and joining with friends to send it around the world to whomever you wish.

PLANTING PRAYER IN THE HEARTS OF OTHERS

✌

*When you have entirely surrendered, everything you do
will be meditation.*

YOGASWAMI, *POSITIVE THOUGHTS FOR DAILY MEDITATION*

THE BASIS FOR ALL RELIGIOUSNESS IS THE ULTIMATE ARRIVAL of compassion for oneself and for others. We have discussed the methods needed for us to find acceptance of ourselves, of a compassionate understanding of how we live our own lives, and an awareness of all our so-called faults and virtues. Until this is accomplished it is hard for us to feel the same way about others, for self-knowledge brings universal knowledge. By knowledge we are not talking about mathematics or science, history, or geography, but an inner comprehension of the human soul and its needs within our own bodies and minds.

Essentially, human beings are all alike. There may be personality differences on the surface, but this is purely superficial and, ultimately, at least within the spiritual quest, of little importance except to the ego. What lie beneath are the same fears, needs, love, doubts, and certainties shared by all. If we comprehend our own needs—for love from others, for security, joy, and inspiration—then we immediately understand that everyone else is the same. In understanding this we can care for it, because if we forgive our own prejudices, anxieties, and doubts, we can begin to forgive those same traits in the rest of the human race.

This does not mean that we have to become involved in charitable works or become priests, for we can, as we understand our own lives, choose whom we share them with. The understanding of personal needs brings a capacity to select the individuals with whom we find solace and delight. As we learn self-love, so we also learn the measure of our companions more easily. We can learn to allow others their failings rather than hate them for their differences. The opposite of this is the whole basis for human aggression and war. We form a judgment about religious creed, color, language, or sex, and combine it with our conditioned suspicion of everything that appears different from us, so we make war. This war does not exist purely on national or religious differences. This war exists in the streets every day, in traffic, tense days, neighborhood conflicts, at work, in the home, in relationships, and in the most petty struggles that we choose to undertake. And we do choose to undertake them. It is never that they happen to us without our input. Our internal struggle gives rise to conflict on the outside. If you hate yourself, then you will hate the world or some part of it, and as a direct result, it will hate you back, for sure. This is a universal truth.

We can think of ourselves as being the apex of a circle that emanates from the middle of the forehead (what the Eastern religions call the third eye) and stretches out into the universe. This circle spins outward and forms what Albert Einstein described as the eternal curve, then travels forever into existence and returns directly into the back of the head. What we have inside travels out from the front and hits us like a boomerang in the back of the neck. And it happens instantly, because in these matters there is no time lapse. We do not need to wait for lifetimes to receive the benefits or problems of our negative thoughts. They come back to us in the instant—in our anxiety, pain, suffering, and doubt, even in the actions of others toward us—for if we are suspicious of the words and deeds of others, so this same distrust echoes in their apparent actions toward us. Trust lies in our own hearts, not in others' actions.

We aren't suggesting that you should go out and love everyone, hug people in the street, or kiss your neighbor or your boss. The process of human compassion does not mean giving flowers and smiling at everyone as the youth of the 1960s suggested. And it's not necessary to accompany compassionate behavior with acetic Puritanism. Compassion is simply understanding, and that understanding merely brings relaxation in the individual that knows it. If you can relax with others, you can also love them, and this love may simply include a silence and a sharing of your gift with those around you or an unconscious power to motivate others with the energy that results from your inner relaxation, rather than a constant output of anxiety and anger or fear. Anger and anxiety are, after all, exhausting.

The less fear there develops in the world, the greater the peace that will follow, and prayer is a great method of planting this joy in others.

The prayer can, of course, be spoken in the silence of your personal temple or shared in a group prayer circle. It can be simply a warmth when you meet someone new or when a new member of staff arrives in your office or factory. It can be a gesture or even just a smile to a stranger rather than a scowl or cool empty expression.

Planting of prayer in the hearts of others occurs through the gesture of a warm heart, a heart that has learned and understood compassion through self-knowledge. And self-knowledge arises out of acceptance of what you are. This concept is common to all religions. There is no need to examine it, analyze it, or scientifically dissect it. There is only a need to watch what happens to you every day. Watch, for example, when you stand in a bus line and someone pushes ahead of you. Watch how you feel anger immediately and indignation at the thought, "How can this person think he has the right?" Your anger is not his fault. It is not your fault either. It simply exists there alongside the rest, and it is you that it hurts, never the other. For if you push the other, it will be his anger that will hurt him, not yours.

Emotions such as anger actually cause an electrical reaction within the body, an injection of chemicals such as adrenaline, that boost the body into a state of turmoil. We are so accustomed to these "injections" that we take them totally for granted, especially if we live in big cities where the very air is full of anger. The body is kicked around all day long by adverse emotional responses, and any attempt at a calm and fulfilling day is almost impossible, because we immediately identify with the mind's blame for the outside cause of the emotional response. In such a life, how can we feel compassion? We are too exhausted by the stimuli that occur around us.

But if, when the man barges to the head of the line, we simply accept our anger as a habit, if we stop and say to ourselves, "Here is anger again, rising in me, as usual," and do nothing about it—divert the mind onto another habit, a habit of acceptance of this state—we defuse the emotional physical response after only a little practice. It's a little like an act of magic when this begins to work, for we feel better about ourselves, about the person who seemed to be the cause of it, and about life in general. Let the others yell at him and push. They are going to suffer, not you. Allow the guy the benefit of the doubt. Perhaps he is in a terrible hurry. Perhaps he is simply unhappy with himself generally. He is a person to be sorry for, not angry with. Let him be, for it doesn't really matter anyway, even if he does get on the bus before you. Street traffic would benefit enormously by this prayer planted into the heart of others, for this act of self-acceptance and awareness is nothing more or less than a prayer.

And if you need a mantra for such situations, you will find many in the section later in this book on prayers for others. Or simply say, "I accept the need of my personal pain, and I have no need to pass it onto others, for they have sufficient of their own. I wish this person well."

So our journey through the practices and variations of prayer is done. The following pages look into the prayers themselves and then the places where prayer most frequently occurs.

PART TWO

A Gathering
of Prayers

ᕫᕬ

I must realize
That my God-satisfaction
Is only a prayer away.
Therefore, let me embark
On my prayer-journey
Lovingly and confidently.
SRI CHINMOY

THE SPIRITUAL PRACTICE
OF PRAYER

ↄ

And in that day ye shall ask me nothing. Verily, verily, I say unto you,
Whatsoever ye shall ask the Father in my name, He will give it to you.
Hitherto have ye asked nothing in my name;
ask, and ye shall receive, that your joy may be full.

JOHN 16:23–24

This section contains prayers organized by theme culled from all
world religious and spiritual traditions and all periods of history.

PRAYERS FOR
SOCIAL OCCASIONS

Listen to the salutation to the dawn,
Look to this day for it is life, the very life of life,
In its brief course lie all the verities and realities of our existence.
The bliss of growth, the splendor of beauty,
For yesterday is but a dream and tomorrow is only a vision,
But today well spent makes every yesterday a dream of happiness and
*   every tomorrow a vision of hope.*
Look well therefore to this day.
Such is the salutation to the dawn.

SANSKRIT SALUTATION TO THE DAWN

The earth is the Lord's and the fullness thereof;
The world, and they that dwell therein.
For it is He who founded it upon the seas,
And established it upon the floods.
Who may ascend the mountain of the Lord,
And who may stand in His holy place?
He that has clean hands and a pure heart,
Who sets not his heart upon falsehood,
Nor swears deceitfully.
He will receive a blessing from the Lord,
And help from the God of his deliverance.
Such is the generation of them that seek Him, O Jacob,
Of them that seek His Presence.
Lift up your heads, O gates,
And be lifted up, you everlasting doors,
That the King of glory may enter.
Who is the King of Glory?
The Lord strong and mighty,
The Lord mighty in battle,
Lift up your heads, O gates,
Lift them up, you everlasting doors,
That the King of glory may enter.
Who is the King of glory?
The Lord of all creation;
He is the King of glory.

PSALM 24

May thy peace and serenity bless us and the light of thy countenance shine upon our pathway henceforth and forever.

In the silence may we feel the holy presence of God, our Creator.

We open our hearts to the incoming of the light of God, praying that we may feel the impress of God's love drawing us all together in one spirit—those who are in the physical body, and the hosts in the world unseen.

We pray that we may realize this at-one-ment of spirit, and that during this service thy love may rise within our hearts and go out to all mankind, to all creation.

O gracious Spirit, we thank thee in humility for the expanding consciousness of thy goodness, thy love, in our hearts; and we thank thee for the knowledge of thy love and thy power to permeate our lives and lift them to thy world of beauty.

WHITE EAGLE

Day of Light,
Day of birth,
Here is God
Come to earth.

JOANNA M. WESTON, CHRISTMAS PRAYER

The living God we praise, exalt, adore;
He was; He is; He will be evermore.
No unity like unto His can be;
Eternal, inconceivable is He.
No form or shape has the incorporeal One,
Most holy, beyond comparison.
He was ere aught was made in heaven or earth;
But His existence has no date or birth.

THE KADDISH, PRAYERS FOR THE PILGRIM FESTIVALS

A new year is approaching;
What does it hold for me?
It may bring joy or sorrow;
Oh, God, what shall it be?
Sometimes my heart is anxious—
I think that I should know
The way into the future—
Each step that I will go.
But You, in Your great wisdom
Must plan for me my all
Lest as Your child I falter
And miss Your perfect call.
Dear Lord, I pray for guidance
In all I say and do,
And then the year upcoming
Will truly honor You!

MILDRED M. SMITH, PRAYER FOR NEW YEAR'S EVE

When the state of dreaming has dawned,
Do not lie in ignorance like a corpse,
Enter the natural sphere of unwavering attentiveness.
Recognize your dreams and transform illusion into luminosity.
Do not sleep like an animal.
Do the practice which mixes sleep and reality.

TIBETAN BUDDHIST PRAYER, SPIRITUAL DREAM PRAYER
BEFORE SLEEP

Thank you very, very much;
my God, thank you.
Give me food today,
food for my sustenance every day.
Thank you very, very much.

SAMBURU (KENYA)

May the Lord accept this, our offering, and bless our food that it may
bring us strength in our body, vigor in our mind, and selfless devotion
in our hearts for His service.

SWAMI PARAMANANDA

Now that I am about to eat, O Great Spirit, give my thanks to the
beasts and birds whom You have provided for my hunger; and pray de-
liver my sorrow that living things must make a sacrifice for my comfort
and well-being.

Let the feather of corn spring up in its time and let it not wither but
make full grains for the fires of our cooking pots, now that I am about
to eat.

NATIVE AMERICAN GRACE

We come to join in the banquet of love. Let it open our hearts and
break down the fears that keep us from loving each other.

DOMINICAN GRACE

This ritual is one.
The food is one.
We who offer the food are one.
The fire of hunger is also one.
All action is one.
We who understand this are one.

HINDU PRAYER FOR MEALS

PRAYERS FOR AND OF THE SAINTS

May the road rise to meet you,
may the wind be always at your back,
may the sun shine warm on your face,
the rain fall softly on your fields;
and until we meet again,
may God hold you in the palm of his hand.

GAELIC PRAYER FOR SAINT PATRICK'S DAY

O my Lady, the holy Virgin Mary, thou has been likened to many things, yet there is nothing which compares with thee. Neither heaven can match thee, nor the earth equal as much as the measure of thy womb. For thou didst confine the Unconfinable, and carry him whom none has power to sustain.

The cherubim are but thy Son's chariot bearers, and even the seraphim bow down in homage at the throne of thy Firstborn. How sublime is the honor of thy royal estate.

O holy Virgin, instrument of our strength and power, our grace, deification, joy, and fortune; glory of our human race! Thou wast the means whereby the salvation of the world was accomplished, and through whom God was reconciled to the sons of mankind. And it was through thee that created human nature was united an indivisible union with the Divine Being of the Creator.

What an unheard-of thing for the potter to clothe himself in a clay vessel, or the craftsman in a handicraft. What humility beyond words for the Creator to clothe himself in the body of a human creature.

And now I cry unto thy Son, O Virgin, saying:

O thou who hast preferred the humble estate of men to the high rank of angels, do not reject thy servant because of the sins I have committed.

Thou whose desire was to partake of earthly rather than heavenly beings, let me share in the secret of thy flawless Divine Being.

Thou to whom Jacob was more comely than Esau, do not scorn me because of my transgressions. For against thee only I have sinned, and much sin have I heaped upon me.

Thou didst create me pure and righteous, yet of my own will I became unclean, and through the persuasion of the wicked one went astray. Thou didst adorn me with gifts of priceless worth which I cast away in favor of unrighteousness.

Make speed, O Lord, to build me into a fortress for the Holy Spirit, Raise me up lest I crumble into a desolate ruin of sin. Make speed to forgive for forgiveness is with thee.

O Lord thou knowest the balm to heal my wounds, the help to strengthen my weakness, the path to prosper my progress. Thou knowest all that is expedient to fulfill my life, as the potter knows how to contrive his own vessel's perfection. For the work is wrought according to the design and wisdom of its maker.

ETHIOPIAN PRAYER TO THE VIRGIN MARY

I am happy
When I pray to the secret God.
I am happier
When I pray to the sacred God.
I am happiest
When I pray to the compassionate God.

SRI CHINMOY

O Lord God, Eternal King! You who stretched out the heavens and built the earth. You who put limits on the ocean and trampled the Serpent's head. You, O Lord, so not abandon me now. Hear my prayer.

SAINT PRISCA

O Lord,
I place myself in your hands and dedicate myself to you.
I pledge myself to do your will in all things—
To love the Lord God with all my heart, all my soul, all my strength.
Not to kill, not to steal, not to covet, not to bear false witness,
    to honor all persons.
Not to do to another what I should not want done to myself.
Not to seek after pleasures. To love fasting. To relieve the poor.
To clothe the naked. To visit the sick. To bury the dead.
To help in trouble. To console the sorrowing.
To hold myself aloof from worldly ways.
To prefer nothing to the love of Christ.
Not to give way to anger.
Not to foster a desire for revenge.
Not to entertain deceit in the heart.
Not to make a false peace.
Not to forsake charity.
Not to swear, lest I swear falsely.
To speak the truth with heart and tongue.
Not to return evil for evil.
To do no injury, indeed, even to bear patiently any injury done to me.
To love my enemies.
Not to curse those who curse me but rather to bless them.
To bear persecution for justice's sake.
Not to be proud.
Not to be given to intoxicating drink.
Not to be an overeater.
Not to be lazy.
Not to be slothful.
Not to be a detractor.
To put my trust in God.
To refer the good I see in myself to God.
To refer any evil I see in myself to myself.
To fear the day of judgment.
To be in dread of hell.

To desire eternal life with spiritual longing.

To keep death before my eyes daily.

To keep constant watch over my actions.

To remember that God sees me everywhere.

To call upon Christ for defense against evil thoughts that arise in my heart.

To guard my tongue against wicked speech.

To avoid much speaking.

To avoid idle talk.

Not to seek to appear clever.

To read only what is good to read.

To pray often.

To ask forgiveness daily for my sins, and to seek ways to amend my life.

To obey my superiors in all things rightful.

Not to desire to be thought holy, but to seek holiness.

To fulfill the commandments of God by good works.

To love chastity.

To hate no one.

Not be jealous or envious of anyone.

Not to love strife.

Not to love pride.

To honor the aged.

To pray for my enemies.

To make peace after a quarrel, before the setting of the sun.

Never to despair of your mercy, O God of Mercy.

SAINT BENEDICT

Lord Jesus, bind us to you and to our neighbor with love.
May our hearts not be turned away from you.
May our souls not be deceived nor our talents or minds enticed by
*   allurements or error,*
*   so that we may never distance ourselves from your love.*
Thus may we love our neighbor as ourselves with strength, wisdom,
*   and gentleness.*
With your help, you who are blessed throughout all ages.

SAINT ANTHONY OF PADUA

Christ be with me, Christ before me, Christ behind me,
Christ in me, Christ beneath me, Christ above me,
Christ on my right, Christ on my left,
Christ where I lie, Christ where I sit, Christ where I arise,
Christ in the heart of every one who thinks of me,
Christ in the mouth of every one who speaks of me,
Christ in every eye that sees me,
Christ in every ear that hears me.
Salvation is of the Lord.
Salvation is of the Christ.
May your salvation, Lord, be ever with us.

SAINT PATRICK

Lord, You must give us this new house. We need it. And I have nobody
to look to but You, dear Lord!

BLESSED ROSE HAWTHORNE LATHROP

Lord, I cannot do this unless You enable me.

BROTHER LAWRENCE

O, Jesus, watch over me always, especially today, or I shall betray you like Judas.

SAINT PHILIP NERI

Jesus, destroy this chain of a body, for I shall never be content until my soul can fly to you. When shall I be completely blessed in you?

SAINT GEMMA GALGANI

This morning my soul is greater than the world since it possesses You, You whom heaven and earth do not contain.

SAINT MARGARET OF CORTONA

PRAYERS FOR HOME, FAMILY MEMBERS, AND FRIENDS

Who was it that bore us in the womb,
and carried such a treasure, day by day?
Was it you that took the pain and cried,
'til we saw the first break of day?
Who nursed us, bathed us, dressed us,
sang lullabies to ease life's pain,
and when we cried, tenderly caressed us,
'til peaceful slumber came again?
Who stitched and sewed, and ironed all night,
so we could proudly stroll to school?
And who also taught us wrong from right,
spared the rod, and used the "Golden Rule"?
Who scrubbed the floors, cooked our meals,
and labored hard each and every day,
just so we would know how it feels,
to enjoy our childhood's play?
Who sacrificed, and did without,
so we would know no shame,
and many times, took Father's clout,
when really, we were to blame?
As time went by, we spread our wings,
and oft' we were apt to go astray;
but, as we went out to "do our things,"
whose watchful eye was there to guide our way?
The years have flown swiftly by,
and time has made us much the wiser,
as now we raise our glasses high,
who here cannot now praise her?
Thank you, Mother Dear—please hear us!

THOMAS K. HYLAND, JR., PRAYER FOR MOTHER'S DAY

Little Man how fast you grew
And went the way all children do
Into a world you've yet to know,
You needed room to stretch and grow.
I watched with pride as you felt your way
And tested strengths in work and play.
We shared our fun as buddies do—
When you were cut, I bled some, too.
Shooting the rapids or climbing high,
Gazing at stars in a western sky;
We gave it our best just like a team,
A young man's game—an old man's dream.
I'll always treasure those memories past,
Could prayers but make the good times last.
But boys were meant to grow up strong
And daddies can't just tag along.
So I hope you know and understand
I'm always near if you need a hand,
And all God's gifts could I choose but one . . .
It would be a father's love for his son.

C. DAVID HAY, PRAYER FOR FATHER'S DAY

I cleanse my soul in the dews of Spring,
light of mind's refreshing dew,
love of heart's renewing dew,
life being's restoring dew,
cleanse and re-create my soul this night.
May the souls of all beings be
peacefully preserved
from fall of night
till day's dear light.

CELTIC

They've added a new holiday, Lord, a day to honor the grandparents who tended us so well. Pause with us as we play again in the dusty lanes of childhood at Grandma and Grandpa's house; as we realize again that we are so special that you gave us these bigger-than-life companions to help bridge home and away, childhood and maturity. In their footsteps, we made the journey. Thank you for such a heritage.

MARGARET ANNE HUFFMAN, PRAYER FOR GRANDPARENTS

My heart is filled with joy when I see you here, as the brooks fill with water when the snows melt in the spring, and I feel glad, as the ponies are when the fresh grass starts in the beginning of the year.

I heard of your coming, when I was many sleeps away, and I made but few camps before I met you. I knew that you had come to do good to me and to my people. I look for the benefits, which would last forever, and so my face shines with joy, as I look upon you.

TEN BEARS, PRAYER OF WELCOME

Oh, the comfort, the inexpressible comfort of feeling safe with a person, having neither to weigh thought nor measure words, but pouring them all right out, just as they are, chaff and grain together, certain that a faithful hand will take and sift them, keep what is worth keeping, and with a breath of kindness, blow the rest away.

ANONYMOUS (SHOSHONE)

May the house wherein I dwell be blessed;
My good thoughts here possess me;
May my path of life be straight and true;
My dreams as here I lie be joyous;
All above, below, about me
May the house I love be hallowed.

FROM OMAHA, NEBRASKA

Lord, behold our family here assembled.
We thank you for this place in which we dwell,
for the love that unites us,
for the peace accorded us this day,
for the hope with which we expect the morrow;
for the health, the work, the food and the bright skies
that make our lives delightful;
for our friends in all parts of the earth. Amen.

ROBERT LOUIS STEVENSON

O merciful Father, we recall before Thee, each one of us, those who are
nearest and dearest to us: mother, father, wife, husband, son, daughter,
friend. In the quiet of the sanctuary, the names and the qualities of
them all are counted over with tender longing. Each capacity, each
merit, and each grace shines before us now as a crown to a treasured
name and as an incentive to rich and noble living.

THE KADDISH, MORNING SERVICE

My father built,
And his father built,
And I have built.
Leave me to live here in success,
Let me sleep in comfort,
And have children.
There is food for you.

UGANDAN

This bed I make
In the name of the Father, and of the Son,
and of the Holy Spirit;
In the name of the night we were conceived;
In the name of the day we were baptized;
In the name of every night, every day, every season,
And of every angel that is in Heaven.

GAELIC PRAYER FOR SANCTIFYING THE BED

O eternal God, who alone makest man to be of one mind in a house;
Help us, the members of this household, faithfully to fulfill our duties to
thee and to each other.
Put far from us all unkind thoughts, anger, and evil speaking.
Give us tender hearts, full of affection and sympathy toward all.
Grant us grace to feel the sorrows and trials of others as our own, and to
bear patiently with their imperfections.
Preserve us from selfishness, and grant that, day by day, walking in love,
we may grow up into the likeness of thy blessed Son, and be found ready
to meet him, and to enter with him into that place which he has gone
to prepare for us;
for his sake, who liveth and reigneth with thee and the Holy Ghost, one
God, world without end.

CHRISTIAN PRAYER TO BLESS THE HOME

PRAYERS FOR GUIDANCE

Grant me, O Lord,
to know what I ought to know,
to love what I ought to love,
to praise what delights you most,
to value what is precious in your sight,
to hate what is offensive to you.
Do not allow me to judge according to the sight of my eyes,
nor to pass sentence according to the hearing of the ears of ignorant men;
but to discern with a true judgment between things visible and
spiritual, and above all things, always to inquire what is the good plea-
sure of your will.

THOMAS À KEMPIS

O gracious and holy Father,
Give us wisdom to perceive you,
intelligence to understand you,
diligence to seek you,
patience to wait for you,
eyes to see you,
a heart to meditate on you,
and a life to proclaim you,
through the power of the spirit of Jesus Christ
our Lord.

SAINT BENEDICT

Teach me to seek thee, and reveal thyself to me when I seek thee, for I
cannot seek thee except thou teach me, nor find thee, except thou reveal
thyself.

SAINT ANSELM

We are what we think.
All that we are arises with our thoughts.
With our thoughts we make the world.
Speak or act with an impure mind
and trouble will follow you,
As the wheel follows the ox that draws the cart.
Speak or act with a pure mind
and happiness will follow you,
As your shadow, unshakeable.

THE DHAMMAPADA, SAYINGS OF THE BUDDHA

May God the Father who made us bless us
May God the Son send his healing among us
May God the Holy Spirit move within us and give us
eyes to see with, ears to hear with and hands
that your work might be done.
May we walk and preach the word of God to all.
May the angel of peace watch over us and lead us at last by God's grace
    to the Kingdom.

DOMINICAN

Go placidly amid the noise and haste and remember what peace there
may be in silence.
As far as possible without surrender be on good terms with all persons.
Speak your truth quietly and clearly and listen to others, even the dull
and ignorant; they, too, have their story.
Avoid loud and aggressive persons, they are vexations to the spirit.
If you compare yourself with others, you may become vain and bitter
for always there will be greater and lesser persons than yourself.
Enjoy your achievements as well as your plans.
Keep interested in your own career, however humble; it is a real posses-
sion in the changing fortunes of time.

Exercise caution in your business affairs, for the world is full of trickery.

But let this not blind you to what virtue there is; many persons strive for high ideals; and everywhere life if full of heroism.

Be yourself. Especially, do not feign affection. Neither be cynical about love; for in the face of all aridity and disenchantment it is perennial as grass.

Take kindly the counsel of the years, gracefully surrendering the things of youth. Nurture strength of spirit to shield you in sudden misfortune. But do not distress yourself with imaginings. Many fears are born of fatigue and loneliness. Beyond a wholesome discipline, be gentle with yourself.

You are a child of the universe, no less than the trees and the stars; you have a right to be here.

Whatever your labors and aspirations, in the noisy confusion of life keep peace with your soul. With all its shame, drudgery and broken dreams, it is still a beautiful world.

Be cheerful.

Strive to be happy.

ANONYMOUS, KNOWN AS THE DESIDERATA

Freedom from fear, purity of heart, constancy in sacred learning and contemplation, generosity, self-harmony, adoration, study of the scriptures, austerity, righteousness;

Nonviolence, truth, freedom from anger, renunciation, serenity, aversion to fault-finding, sympathy for all beings, peace from greedy cravings, gentleness, modesty, steadiness;

Energy, forgiveness, fortitude, purity, a good will, freedom from pride—these are the treasures of the man who is born for heaven.

Deceitfulness, insolence and self-conceit, anger and harshness, and ignorance—these belong to a man who is born for hell.

THE BHAGAVAD GITA

Prefer death to disgrace.
Be content with little
rather than curry favor.
One who would not
receive something anyway
would not get it
by contrivance.
Destiny is two days,
one for you
and one against you,
so when it is for you,
do not be proud or reckless,
and when it is against you,
then be patient.
Put aside your pride,
set down your arrogance,
and remember your grave.
Truth will throw down
anyone who fights with it.
The heart is the book
of perception.
Conscience is the head of character.
Endure with the patience
of the free,
or else forget with the forgetfulness
of the ingenious.
Understanding is what makes relationships.

HADRAT 'ALI

Holy Goddess tell us,
Mother of Living Nature,
The food of life
Thou meter out in eternal loyalty
And, when life has left us,
We take our refuge in Thee.
Thus everything Thou dolest out
Returns into Thy womb.
Rightly Thou art called Mother of the Gods
Because by Thy loyalty
Thou hast conquered the power of the gods.
Verily Thou art also the Mother
Of the peoples and the gods,
Without Thee nothing can thrive nor be;
Thou art powerful, of the gods Thou art
The Queen and also the Goddess.
Thee, Goddess, and Thy power I now invoke;
Thou canst easily grant all that I ask,
And in exchange I will give Thee, Goddess, sincere thanks.

EULOGY (SECOND CENTURY C.E.)

To the Awakened One for refuge I go,
To the Sangha (Community) for refuge I go...
To the Dharma (the Way) for refuge I go.

BUDDHA, THE THREE GREAT SHELTERS

My prayer is but a cold affair, Lord,
because my love burns with so small a flame,
but you who are so rich in mercy
will not mete out to them your gifts
according to the dullness of my zeal,
but as your kindness is above all human love
so let your eagerness to hear
be greater than the feeling in my prayers.
Do this for them and with them, Lord,
so that they may speed according to your will
and thus ruled and protected by you,
always and everywhere,
may they come at last to glory and eternal rest,
through you who are living and reigning God through all ages.

SAINT ANSELM

PRAYERS FOR BIRTH

*From the Heart of Earth, by means of yellow pollen blessing is
  extended.*
From the Heart of Sky, by means of blue pollen blessing is extended.
On top of a pollen floor may I there in blessing give birth!
On top of a floor of fabrics may I there in blessing give birth!
*As collected water flows ahead of it, whereby blessing moves along
  ahead of it, may I there in blessing give birth!*
*Thereby without hesitation, thereby with its mind straightened, thereby
  with its travel means straightened, thereby without its sting, may I
  there in blessing give birth!*
*As water's child glows behind it, whereby blessing moves along behind
  it, may I there in blessing give birth!*
*Thereby without hesitation, thereby with its mind straightened, thereby
  with its travel means straightened, thereby without its sting, may I
  there in blessing give birth!*
*With pollen moving around it, with blessing extended from it by means
  of pollen, may I in blessing give birth!*
*May I give birth to Pollen Boy, may I give birth to Cornbeetle Boy, may
  I give birth to Long-life Boy, may I give birth to Happiness Boy!*
*With long-life-happiness surrounding me, may I in blessing give birth!
  May I quickly give birth!*
*In blessing may I arise again, in blessing may I recover, as one who is
  long-life-happiness, may I live on!*
*Before me may it be blessed, behind me may it be blessed, below me
  may it be blessed, above me may it be blessed, in all surroundings
  may it be blessed, may my speech be blessed!*
*It has become blessed again, it has become blessed again, it has
  become blessed again, it has become blessed again!*

NAVAJO BIRTH CHANT

in the house with the tortoise chair she will give birth to the pearl to the
*   beautiful feather*
in the house of the goddess who sits on a tortoise she will give birth to
*   the necklace of pearls to the beautiful feathers we are*
there she sits on the tortoise
swelling to give us birth
on your way on your way
child be on your way to me here
you whom I made new
come here child
come be pearl be beautiful feather

ANSELM HOLLO, AZTEC PRAYER FOR BIRTH

Here am I,
myself,
but also vessel of creation.
Rhythms of the ages stir the Womb of Woman,
my own womb—
ancient pulse in my own heartbeat,
nourishment in my own breast.
This life through me was fathered deep
in fire-consecrated flesh, and here, behold!
A miracle, that what was not before
is
now!

NANCY ROSE MEEKER

That she was taken out of her mother, thanks be for that!
That she, the little one, was taken out of her, we say, thanks be for that!

GREENLAND ESKIMO CHANT FOR BIRTH

My sun!
My morning star!
Help this child to become a man.
I name him
Rain-dew Falling!
I name him
Star Mountain!

NATIVE AMERICAN TEWA BIRTH PRAYER

Creator of the germ in woman,
Maker of seed in man,
Giving life to the son in the body of his mother,
Soothing him that he may not weep,
Nurse in the womb,
Giver of breath to animate every one that he maketh!
When he cometh forth from the womb . . . on the day of his birth,
Thou openest his mouth in speech,
Thou suppliest his necessities.
When the fledgling in the egg chirps in the shell
Thou givest him breath therein to preserve him alive. . . .
He goeth about upon his two feet
When he hath come forth therefrom.
How manifold are thy works!
They are hidden from before us
O sole God, whose powers no other possesseth.
Thou didst create the earth according to thy heart.

IKHNATON, PHARAOK'S HYMN TO THE SUN (ANCIENT
EGYPT)

O Muumbi,
You who have created
All human beings,
You have conferred
A great benefit on us
By bringing us this child.

KAMBA (KENYA)

Dear Father,
Hear and Bless
Your beasts
And singing birds:
And guard with tenderness
Small things
That have no words.

ANONYMOUS

PRAYERS FOR LOVE AND LOVERS

The essence of beauty
springs
from the eternal play
of man as Krishna
and woman as Radha.
Devoted lovers
in the act of loving
seek to reach
the goal.

PRAYER OF THE SAHAJIYAS (INDIA)

But the true servants of God shall be well provided for, feasting on fruit,
and honored in the gardens of delight. Reclining face to face upon soft
couches, they shall be served with a goblet filled at a gushing fountain,
white, and delicious to those who drink it. It will neither dull their
senses nor befuddle them. They shall sit with bashful, dark-eyed virgins,
as chaste as the sheltered eggs of ostriches.

THE QUR'AN

Honey bee, Krishna's flute is honey-sweet.
We hear, and our very breath is immersed in love
like a wick immersed in oil,
shining hot and bright,
And the moths see the flame,
and destroy their greedy bodies;
like a fish who yearns for a silver meat,
and seizes a bamboo hook;
a crooked thorn,
It twists in the heart
and then will not come out.
As a hunter sounds a horn
and draws a herd of deer;
Aims an arrow,
looses it
and threads their hearts upon the shaft.
As a thug lures a pilgrim
with laddus sweet with wine,
Makes him drunk and trusting,
takes his money and his life;
Just so, Honey bee,
Hari takes our love by deceit.
Sur's lord tore up the sweet sugar-cane
and planted a garden of longing.

KRISHNA, LOVERS PRAYER (INDIA)

I set up house for You in my heart
As a friend that I could talk with.
I gave my body to someone else
Who wanted to embrace it.
This body, all in all, is good enough for embracing—
But the friend who lives in my house
Is the lover of my heart.
I have two ways of loving You:
A selfish one
And another way that is worthy of You.
In my selfish love, I remember You and You alone.
In that other love, You lift the Veil
And let me feast my eyes on Your living Face.
That I remember You always, or that I see You face-to-face—
No credit to me in either:
The credit is to You in both.
If you hadn't singled me out to suffer Your love,
I never would've brought You
All these lovers—
(Lord Remember!)

RABI'A AL-ADAWIYYA

I am mad with love
And no one understands my plight.
Only the wounded
Understand the agonies of the wounded,
When a fire rages in the heart.

MIRA BAI

*O gracious amiable Blessedness and great Love, how sweet art thou!
How friendly and courteous art thou! How pleasant and lovely is thy
relish and taste! How ravishing sweetly dost thou smell! O noble Light,
and bright Glory, who can apprehend thy exceeding beauty? How
comely adorned is thy love! How curious and excellent are thy colors!
And all this eternally. Who can express it?*

*Or why and what do I write, whose tongue does but stammer like a
child which is learning to speak? With what shall I compare it? Or to
what shall I liken it? Shall I compare it with the love of this world? No,
that is but a mere dark valley to it.*

*O immense Greatness! I cannot compare thee with any thing, but only
with the resurrection from the dead; there will the Love-Fire rise up
again in us, and rekindle again our astringent, bitter, and cold, dark,
and dead powers, and embrace us most courteously and friendly.*

*O gracious, amiable, blessed Love and clear bright Light, tarry with us,
I pray thee, for the evening is at hand.*

JAKOB BÖHME

*My kingdom of love shall expand. I have loved my body more than
anything else. That is why I am identified with and limited by it. With
the love that I have given to the body, I will love all those who love me,
I will love those who are mine. With the love for myself and the love for
my own, I will love those who are strangers. I will use all my love to
love those who do not love me, as well as those who love me. I will
bathe all souls in my unselfish love. In the sea of my love, my family
members, my countrymen, all nations, and all beings will swim. All
creation, all the myriads of tiny living things, will dance on the waves
of my love.*

PARAMAHANSA YOGANANDA

Wild Nights—Wild Nights!
Were I with thee
Wild Nights should be
Our luxury!
Futile—the Winds—
To a Heart in port—
Done with the Compass—
Done with the Chart!
Rowing in Eden—
Ah, the Sea!
Might I but moor—Tonight—
In Thee!

EMILY DICKINSON

Come then, your ways and airs and looks, locks, maiden gear, gallantry and gaiety and grace,

Winning ways, airs innocent, maiden manners, sweet looks, loose locks, long locks, lovelocks, gaygear, going gallant, girl-grace—

Resign them, sign them, seal them, send them, motion them with breath,

And with sighs soaring, soaring sighs deliver

Them; beauty-in-the-ghost, deliver it, early now, long before death

Give beauty back, beauty, beauty, beauty, back to God, beauty's self and beauty's giver.

GERARD MANLEY HOPKINS

O God, the stars are shining:
All eyes have closed in sleep;
The kings have locked their doors.
Each lover is alone, in secret, with the one he loves,
And I am here, too: alone, hidden from all of them—
With You.

RABI'A AL-ADAWIYYA

Give me the Pain of Love, the Pain of Love for Thee!
Not the Joy of Love, just the Pain of Love,
And I will pay the price, any price you ask!
All myself I will offer for it, and the price you will ask on top of it!
Keep the Joy for others, give me the Pain,
And gladly will I pay for the Pain of Love!

ANONYMOUS, SUFI

Oh, how I love the memory
Of blessed days in infancy—
My innocence a flower He guarded . . . He
Surrounded me, the Lord above
With love!
Yes, I was little: nonetheless
My heart was filled with tenderness—
This love it had, it could not but express:
My promise to the King of Heav'n
Was giv'n!

SAINT THERESE OF LISIEUX

PRAYERS FOR SPIRITUAL ASPIRATION

Throughout all lifetimes, wherever I am born,
May I obtain the seven qualities of birth in a higher realm;
May I meet the Dharma (divine knowledge) after taking birth,
And have the freedom to practice accordingly.
May I please the venerable spiritual masters
And practice Dharma, and accomplishing its inmost essence,
May I traverse the ocean of worldly existence in that very life.
Within the world may I expound the highest sacred doctrine,
And never become bored, or weary of accomplishing the welfare of the
    others;
And by my own tremendous, impartial service to others
May all beings attain Buddhahood (perfection) together.
              THE DZOGCHEN, PRAYER FOR ASPIRATION (TIBET)

Teach us, Good Lord, to serve Thee as Thou deservest,
To give and not to count the cost;
To fight, and not to heed the wounds;
To toil, and not to seek for rest;
To labor, and not to ask for any reward,
Save that of knowing that we do Thy will.
                    SAINT IGNATIUS OF LOYOLA

You imagined that you would accomplish this task through your own strength, activity, and effort. This is the wont that I have established: Expend everything your have in Our way. Then Our bounty will come to you. On this endless road, We command you to travel with your own feeble hands and feet. We know that you cannot traverse this way with feet so feeble. Indeed, in a hundred thousand years you will not arrive at the first way station. However, when you travel this road until your legs are exhausted and you fall down flat, until you have no more strength to move forward, then God's grace will take you in its arms.

JALAL AL-DIN RUMI

God is your captain, sail, my Ark!
Though Hell unleash her furies red
Upon the living and the dead,
And turn the earth to molten lead,
And sweep the skies of every mark,
God is your captain, sail, my Ark!
Love is your compass, ply, my Ark!
Go north and south, go east and west
And share with all your treasure chest.
The storm shall bear you on its crest
A light for sailors in the dark.
Love is your compass, ply, my Ark!
Faith is your anchor, ride, my Ark!
Should thunder roar, and lightning dart,
And mountain shake and fall apart,
And men become so faint of heart
As to forget the holy spark,
Faith is your anchor, ride, my Ark!

MIKHAIL NAIMY

I would like the angels of Heaven to be among us.
I would like an abundance of peace.
I would like full vessels of charity.
I would like rich treasures of mercy.
I would like cheerfulness to preside over all.
I would like Jesus to be present.
I would like the three Marys of illustrious renown to be with us.
I would like the friends of Heaven to be gathered around us from all
   parts.
I would like myself to be a rent payer to the Lord;
that I should suffer distress, that he would bestow a good blessing upon
   me.

PRAYER OF SAINT BRIDGID OF IRELAND

My aspiration-heart
Is indeed a gift from god.
My dedication-life
Is indeed my gift to God.

SRI CHINMOY

PRAYERS AND HYMNS FOR CELEBRATIONS

Around the Throne of God a band
Of glorious Angels ever stand;
Bright things they see, sweet harps they hold,
And on their heads are crowns of gold.
Some wait around Him, ready still
To sing His praise and do His Will;
And some, when He commands them, go
To guard His servants here below.
Lord, give Thy Angels every day
Command to guide us on our way,
And bid them every evening keep
Their watch around us while we sleep.
So shall no wicked thing draw near,
To do us harm or cause us fear;
And we shall dwell, when life is past,
With Angels round Thy Throne at last.

J. M. NEALE

Thy dawning is beautiful in the horizon of the sky,
O living Aton, Beginning of life!
When thou risest in the eastern horizon
Thou fillest every land with thy beauty.
Thou art beautiful, great, glittering, high above every land,
Thy rays, they encompass the lands, even all that thou hast made.
Though thou art far away, thy rays are upon earth;
Though thou art on high, thy footprints are the day.

AMENHOTEP IV, HYMN TO ATON, THE CREATOR

Sole likeness, maker of what is,
Sole and only one, maker of what exists.
From whose eyes men issued,
From whose mouth the gods came forth,
Maker of herbs for the cattle,
And the tree of life for mankind.

HYMN TO THE SUN-GOD (ANCIENT EGYPT)

Know, son, that everything in the universe is a pitcher brimming with
*   wisdom and beauty,*
The universe is a drop of the Tigris of His beauty,
this beauty was a Hidden Treasure so full it burst open and made the
earth more radiant than the heavens.

JALAL AL-DIN RUMI

Oh my Queen, Queen of the Universe, the Queen who encompasses the
universe, may he the King, enjoy long days at your holy lap.
Who is supreme in heaven? Thou alone art supreme. Who is supreme on
earth? Thou alone art supreme. Thy will is made known in heaven and
the spirits thereof bow low before thee. Thy will is made known upon
earth and the spirits thereof kiss the ground before thee. . . . Thy mighty
word createth right and ordaineth justice for mankind, and thy power-
ful ordinance reacheth unto the uttermost parts of heaven and earth.
Who can know thy will and who can dispute it? . . . O thou king of
kings whose judgments are inscrutable and whose divinity is
unsurpassed.

SUMERIAN TEXT, PRAYER TO THE MOON-GOD FROM AN
ASSYRIAN TRANSLATION INSCRIBED ON A TABLET IN THE
NINEVEH GALLERY AT THE BRITISH MUSEUM IN LONDON,
QUOTED IN *SACRED BOOKS OF THE WORLD* BY
A. C. BOUQUET

Hear, O Israel: The Lord our God is one Lord.

And thou shalt love the Lord thy God with all thine heart, and with all thy soul, and with all thy might.

And these words, which I command thee this day, shall be in thine heart:

And thou shalt teach them diligently unto thy children, and shalt talk of them when thou sittest in thine house, and when thou walkest by the way, and when thou liest down, and when thou risest up.

Deuteronomy 6:4–7

And the wolf shall dwell with the lamb,
And the leopard shall lie down with the kid;
And the calf and the young lion and the fatling shall be together;
And a little child shall lead them.
And the cow shall graze with the bear;
Their young ones shall lie down together;
And the lion shall eat straw like the ox.
And the sucking child shall play at the hole of the asp,
And the weaned child shall put his hand on the adder's den.
None shall hurt nor destroy in all my holy mountain;
For the earth shall be full of the knowledge of the Lord,
As the waters cover the sea.

Isaiah 11:6–9

We plough the fields, and scatter
The good seed on the land,
But it is fed and water'd
By God's Almighty Hand;
He sends the snow in winter,
The warmth to swell the grain,
The breezes, and the sunshine,
And soft refreshing rain.
All good gifts around us

Are sent from Heav'n above,
Then thank the Lord, O thank the Lord,
For all His love.
He only is the Maker
Of all things near and far;
He paints the wayside flower,
He lights the evening star;
The winds and waves obey Him,
By Him the birds are fed;
Much more to us, His children,
He gives our daily bread.
All good gifts around us
Are sent from Heav'n above,
Then thank the Lord, O thank the Lord,
For all His love.

JANE M. CAMPBELL

The heavens declare the glory of God; and the firmament showeth his
  handiwork.
Day unto day uttereth speech, and night unto night showeth
  knowledge.
There is no speech nor language, where their voice is not heard.
The line is gone out through all the earth and their words to the end of
  the world. In them hath he set a tabernacle for the sun,
Which is as a bridegroom coming out of his chamber, and rejoiceth as
  a strong man to run a race.
His going forth is from the end of the heaven, and his circuit unto the
  ends of it: and there is nothing hid from the heat thereof.
The law of the Lord is perfect, converting the soul; the testimony of the
  Lord is sure, making wise the simple.
The statutes of the Lord are right, rejoicing the heart: the
  commandment of the Lord is pure, enlightening the eyes.
The fear of the Lord is clean, enduring for ever: the judgments of the
  Lord are true and righteous altogether.
More to be desired are they than God, yea, than much fine gold: sweeter
  also than honey and the honeycomb.
Moreover by them is thy servant warned: and in keeping of them there
  is great reward.
Who can understand his errors: cleanse thou me from secret faults.
Keep back thy servant also from presumptuous sins; let them not have
  dominion over me: then shall I be upright, and I shall be innocent
  from the great transgression.
Let the words of my mouth, and the meditation of my heart, be accept
  able in thy sight, O Lord, my strength, and my redeemer.

PSALM 19

Your picture Jesus, like a star
Is guiding me! Ah, well You know
Your Features—grace itself they are—
To me, are Heaven here below.
Your weeping . . . that, to Love, appears
As ornament—attractiveness!
I'm smiling while I'm shedding tears
At seeing You in Your distress.
To comfort You, I want to be
Unknown, in loneliness. Below
Your Beauty's veiled, and yet to me
Reveals its Mystery! And, oh,
Would I, to you, were flying free!
Your Face . . . my only Homeland, and
The Kingdom, too, where Love has sway:
And it's my smiling meadowland,
The gentle Sun of every day;
The Lily of the Valley—ah,
It's perfume's Mystery! I'm giv'n
What consolation from afar!—
A foretaste of the Peace of Heav'n.
Your Face, that has such tenderness
Is like a sweet reposeful lyre . . .
Bouquet of Myrrh, I would caress
(Such gentleness do You inspire!),
That safely to my heart I'd press . . .
Your Face . . . ah, only that will be
The wealth I ask as revenue:
I'll hide in it, unceasingly;
Then, Jesus, I'll resemble You!
Imprint in me those traits divine
Your Gentleness of Face imparts;
Holiness, then, will soon be mine—
To you I'll be attracting hearts!
So I can gather souls—it's this,

A golden harvest, I desire—
Consume me; give me soon, in bliss,
That tender burning of Your Fire,
Your lips in an eternal Kiss!

SAINT THERESE OF LISIEUX

All things bright and beautiful,
All creatures great and small,
All things wise and wonderful,
The Lord God made them all.
Each little flower that opens,
Each little bird that sings,
He made their glowing colors,
He made their tiny wings.
The rich man in his castle,
The poor man at his gate,
God made them, high or lowly,
And order'd their estate.
The purple-headed mountain,
The river running by,
The sunset and the morning,
That brightens up the sky.

MRS. ALEXANDER

PRAYERS FOR THE BODY AND MIND

Do not begrudge me my ugly exterior,
you who are lacking all virtue and fairness!
This body's a scabbard,
the soul is the sabre:
in the sabre is action
—not in the scabbard.

JĀMĪ

Do not go to the garden of flowers! O Friend! Go not there,
In your body is the garden of flowers.
Take your seat on the thousand petals of the lotus,
and there gaze on the Infinite Beauty.

KABIR

O Jesus, my feet are dirty. Come even as a slave to me, pour water into
your bowl, come and wash my feet. In asking such a thing I know I am
overbold, but I dread what was threatened when you said to me, "If I
do not wash your feet I have no fellowship with you." Wash my feet
then, because I long for your companionship. And yet, what am I ask-
ing? It was well for Peter to ask you to wash his feet; for him that was
all that was needed for him to be clean in every part. With me it is dif-
ferent; though you wash me now I shall still stand in need of that other
washing, the cleansing you promised when you said, "There is a
baptism I must needs be baptized with."

ORIGEN

Father, thank you for your revelation
about death
and illness
and sorrow.
Thank you for speaking so plainly to us,
for calling us all friends
and hovering over us;
for extending your arms out to us.
We cannot stand on our own;
we fall into death without you.
We fall from faith, left to our own.
We are really friendless without you.
Your extended arms fill us with joy,
expressing love,
love caring and carrying,
asking and receiving our trust.
You have our trust, Father,
and our faith,
with our bodies
and all that we are and possess.
We fear nothing when with you,
safe to stretch out and help others,
those troubled in faith,
those troubled in body.
Father, help us to do with our bodies what we proclaim,
that our faith be known to you
and to others,
and be effective in all the world.

Masai (Tanzania)

Withdraw into yourself and look. And if you do not find yourself beautiful yet, act as does the creator of a statue that is to be made beautiful; he cuts away here, he smoothes there, he makes this line lighter, this other purer, until a lovely face has grown upon his work. So do you also; cut away all that is excessive, straighten all that is crooked, bring light to all that is in shadow; labor to make all one glow of beauty and never cease chiseling your statue until there shall shine out on you from it the godlike splendor of virtue, until you shall see the perfect Goodness established in the stainless shrine.

PLOTINUS

Breathing in, I calm my body.
Breathing out, I smile.
Dwelling in the present moment
I know this is a wonderful moment.

THICH NHAT HANH

O my friend! Remain in solitude with a passion to meet the Lord;
Rid thyself of all grief and be happy.
Be not like the whirlwind; be not baffled or perplexed.
Center thy mind on one point, and be free from all thought.

SARMAD

If there is joy in meditation upon the sun and moon,
the planets and fixed stars are the magic creation of the sun and moon;
make thyself like unto the sun and moon themselves.
If there is joy in meditation upon the mountain,
the fruit-trees are the magic creation of the mountain;
make thyself like unto the mountain itself.
If there is joy in meditation upon thine own mind,
distinctive thought is the magic creation of the mind;
make thyself like unto the mind itself.

MILAREPA, THE MESSAGE OF MILAREPA

Let us lay aside all thought of the material world and seek to make con-
tact with the Source of life. O gracious Spirit, all-enfolding love, light
and life, we come before thee in humility and tranquillity of heart and
mind. May nothing in us prevent us from steeping forward into the
light; and when sorrow and trouble come may we willingly surrender to
thy love and wisdom; knowing that underneath are thine everlasting
arms: for thou art merciful and just and all-loving. May our hearts be
open and minds subdued, waiting to receive the beauty of thy light.

O Father Mother God, we thank thee for thy infinite love. May these
thy children go their way in peace, filled with thy holy spirit. Bless
them, bless them, O Son.

WHITE EAGLE

The Supreme Way is not difficult; it just precludes picking and
    choosing.
Without yearning or loathing, the Way is perfectly apparent,
while even a hairbreadth difference separates heaven and earth.
To see the Way with your own eyes, quit agreeing and disagreeing.
The battling of likes and dislikes—that's the disease of the mind.
Misunderstanding the great mystery, people labor in vain for peace.
Mind has the totality of space: nothing lacking, nothing extra.
It's just selecting and rejecting that make it seem otherwise.
Don't pursue worldly concerns, don't dwell passively in emptiness;
in the peace of absolute identity, confusion vanishes by itself.
Suppressing activity to reach stillness just creates agitation.
Dwelling in such dualities, how can you know identity?
People who don't know identity bog down on both sides—
rejecting form, they get stuck in it, seeking emptiness, turn away
    from it.
The more people talk and ponder, the further they spin out of accord.
Bring gabbing and speculation to a stop, and the whole world opens up
    to you.

SENG-TS'AN

PRAYERS FOR KNOWLEDGE

A journey of a thousand miles must begin with a single step.
The softest things in the world overcome the hardest things in the world.
Non-being penetrates that in which there is no space.
Through this I know the advantage of taking no action.
One may know the world without going out of doors.
One may see the way of Heaven without looking through the windows.
The further one goes, the less one knows.
Therefore the sage knows without going about,
Understands without seeing,
And accomplishes without any action.

         LAO-TZU, *TAO TE CHING*

It is not outer awareness
It is not inner awareness
Nor is it suspension of awareness
It is not knowing
It is not unknowing
Nor is it knowingness itself
It can neither be seen nor understood
It cannot be given boundaries
It is ineffable and beyond thought
It is indefinable
It is known only through becoming it.

         THE *MANDUKYA UPANISHAD* (INDIA)

Who is thy wife? Who is thy son?
The ways of this world are strange indeed.
Whose art thou? When art thou come?
Vast is thy ignorance, my beloved.
Therefore ponder these things and worship the Lord.

SHANKARA (INDIA)

And in the fourth watch of the night Jesus went unto them, walking on
the sea. And when the disciples saw him walking on the sea, they were
troubled, saying, "It is a spirit"; and they cried out of fear. But straight-
way Jesus spake unto them, saying, "Be of good cheer; it is I; be not
afraid." And Peter answered him and said, "Lord if it be thou, bid me
come unto thee on the water." And he said, "Come." And when Peter
was come down out of the ship, he walked on the water, to go to Jesus.
But when he saw the wind boisterous, he was afraid; and beginning to
sink, he cried, saying, "Lord, save me." And immediately Jesus stretched
forth his hand, and caught him, and said unto him, "O thou of little
faith, wherefore didst thou doubt?"

MATTHEW 14:25–31

Let us raise our hearts to the great eternal Light. Our Father God, we
thank thee for the joy of learning, for the light which flows from thee;
we pray, O God, that we may walk in simplicity and humility gather-
ing thy knowledge from the simple experiences of life. So may we live
ever more in harmony with thy divine principles and find peace, the
peace of eternity.

WHITE EAGLE

I have three precious things which
I hold fast and prize.
The first is gentleness; the second is frugality;
the third is humility, which keeps me
from putting myself before others.
Be gentle, and you can be bold;
be frugal, and you can be liberal;
avoid putting yourself before others,
and you can become a leader of men.
Gentleness brings victory to him who attacks,
and safety to him who defends.
Those whom heaven would save,
it fences round with gentleness.
The greatest conquerors are those who
overcome their enemies without strife.

LAO-TZU

I'm too alone in the world, yet not alone enough to make each hour
   holy.
I'm too small in the world, yet not small enough to be simply in your
   presence, like a thing—just as it is.
I want to know my own will and to move with it.
And I want, in the hushed moments when the nameless draws near,
to be among the wise ones—or alone.
I want to mirror your immensity.
I want never to be too weak or too old to bear the heavy, lurching
   image of you.
I want to unfold.
Let no place in me hold itself closed, for where I am closed, I am false.
I want to stay clear in your sight.

RILKE

By much silence,
there comes to be awe.
By justice,
communications increase.
By generosity,
worth grows.
By humility,
blessings come about.
By taking burdens upon oneself,
one attains leadership.
By just behavior,
enemies are overcome.
By forbearance in face of a fool,
helpers against him increase.

HADRAT 'ALI

Dearest Lord, teach me to be generous.
Teach me to serve Thee as Thou deservest;
To give and not to count the cost;
To fight and not to heed the wounds;
To toil and not to seek for reward,
Save that of knowing that
I do Thy will, O God.

SAINT IGNATIUS OF LOYOLA

If you can keep your head when all about you
Are losing theirs and blaming it on you.
If you can trust yourself when all men doubt you
And make allowance for their doubting, too.

RUDYARD KIPLING

Wisdom concealed and treasure hidden—
what is the use of either?
Better a man who hides his folly
than one who hides his wisdom!

ECCLESIASTICUS (OLD TESTAMENT TEXTS NOT INCLUDED
IN THE BIBLE), THE APOCRYPHA

Speak, if you are old—it is your privilege—
but come to the point and do not interrupt the music.
Where entertainment is provided, do not keep up a stream of talk;
it is the wrong time to show off your wisdom.

ECCLESIASTICUS (OLD TESTAMENT TEXTS NOT INCLUDED
IN THE BIBLE), THE APOCRYPHA

PRAYERS FOR CHILDREN

Your children are not your children,
They are the sons and daughters of Life's longing for itself.
They come through you but not from you,
And though they are with you, yet they belong not to you.
You may give them your love but not your thoughts.
For they have their own thoughts.
You may house their bodies but not their souls,
For their souls dwell in the house of tomorrow,
which you cannot visit, not even in your dreams.
You may strive to be like them, but seek not
to make them like you.
For life goes not backward nor tarries with yesterday.
You are the bows from which your children
as living arrows are sent forth.
The archer sees the mark upon the path of the infinite,
and He bends you with His might
that His arrows may go swift and far.
Let your bending in the archer's hand be for gladness;
For even as He loves the arrow that flies,
so He loves the bow that is stable.

KAHLIL GIBRAN

Air, water, and earth,
Of these are we made.
Air like the Guru [Nanak]'s word gives the breath of life
To the babe born to the great mother earth
Sired by the waters.
The day and night our nurses be
That watch over us in our infancy.
In their laps we play.
The world is our playground.

GURU NANAK

O Lord my God, shed the light of your love on my child. Keep him safe
from all illness and all injury. Enter his tiny soul, and comfort him
with your peace and joy. He is too young to speak to me, and to my ears
his cries and gurgles are meaningless nonsense. But to your ears they are
prayers. His cries are cries for your blessing. His gurgles are gurgles of
delight at your grace. Let him as a child learn the way of your
commandments. As an adult let him live the full span of life, serving
your kingdom on earth. And finally in his old age let him die in the
sure and certain knowledge of your salvation. I do not ask that he be
wealthy, powerful or famous. Rather I ask that he be poor in spirit,
humble in action, and devout in worship. Dear Lord, smile upon him.

JOHANN STARCK, CHRISTIAN PRAYER

Now that it's over, Lord, thank You, because both my wife and my little boy are doing fine, I've even seen him already, in one of those incubators, fed and wrinkled and, to me, totally beautiful.

You wouldn't think something that small could be alive, but he is, shaking his midget fists at the world and screaming: Look out, I'm here.

He is here, Lord, all here, yet the world won't look out, and he won't have that glass hothouse to protect him like a rose.

He'll have to grow up, and be stepped on, and stand alone against the rain of knocks the world is always too ready to provide. So be with him, Lord, as I will, at least long enough to see his own image made over in the joy of a first child.

MAX PAULI

We bathe your palms
In showers of wine,
In the crook of the kindling,
In the seven elements,
In the sap of the tree,
In the milk of honey,
We place nine pure, choice gifts
In your clear beloved face:
The gift of form,
The gift of voice,
The gift of fortune,
The gift of goodness,
The gift of eminence,
The gift of charity,
The gift of integrity,
The gift of true nobility,
The gift of apt speech.

GAELIC

Grant me, O merciful God, that I might ardently love,
prudently ponder,
rightly acknowledge,
and perfectly fulfill all that is pleasing to you,
for the praise and glory of your Name.

SAINT THOMAS AQUINAS

Newborn, on the naked sand
Nakedly lay it.
Next to the earth mother,
That it may know her;
Having good thoughts of her, the food giver.
Newborn, we tenderly
In our arms take it,
Making good thoughts.
House-god, be entreated,
That it may grow from childhood to manhood,
Happy, contended;
beautifully walking
The trail to old age.
Having good thoughts of the earth its mother,
That she may give it the fruits of her being.
Newborn, on the naked sand
Nakedly lay it.

GRAND PUEBLOS

PRAYERS FOR CONSCIOUSNESS

All eyes that look on me are my sole eyes;
The one heart that beats within all breasts is mine.
The world's happiness flows through me like wine,
Its million sorrows are my agonies.
Yet all its acts are only waves that pass
Upon my surface; only for ever still
Unborn I set, timeless, intangible:
All things are shadows in my tranquil glass.
My vast transcendence holds the cosmic whirl;
I am hid in it as in the sea a pearl.

AUROBINDO GHOSE (INDIA)

I have thrown from me the whirling dance of mind
And stand now in the spirit's silence free;
Timeless and deathless beyond creature-kind,
The center of my own eternity.
My mind is hushed in a wide and endless light,
My heart a solitude of delight and peace,
My sense ensnared by touch and sound and sight,
My body a point in white infinities.
I am the one Being's sole immobile Bliss:
No one I am, I who am all that is.

AUROBINDO GHOSE (INDIA)

All I am is "seeing" when I see,
All I am is "hearing" when I hear,
All I am is "sentience" when I feel,
All I am is understanding when I know.

WEI WU WEI

Moved by whom does thinking attain its object?
Who directs the function of vital breathing?
Moved by whom do people engage in speaking?
Say what force directs both the sight and hearing,
He, the hearing's Hearer, the thinking's Thinker,
speaking's Speaker, even the breathing's Breather.
Eye of eye. The wise by renouncing find Him;
parting from this World they become immortal.

THE KENA UPANISHAD

I was a prisoner carrying a heavy load of bones and flesh, but I have broken the chains of my muscle-bound body by the power of relaxation. I am free. Now I shall try to go within.

Bewitching scenic beauties, stop your dance before my eyes! Lure not my attention away!

Enchanting melodies, keep not my mind enthralled in the revels of earthly songs!

Haunting sirens of sweet sensations, paralyze not my sacred intuitions by your enticing touch! Let my meditation race for the sweet bower of eternal divine love.

Luring aroma of lilacs, jasmine, and roses, stop not my homeward-marching mind!

These tempting enchantresses of senses are now gone. The cords of flesh are broken. The grip of the senses is loosened. I exhale and stop the storm of breath; the ripples of thought melt away.

I am sitting on the altar of my throbbing heart. I watch the roaring, shouting torrent of life-force moving through the heart into the body. I turn backward to the spine. The beat and roar of the heart are gone. Like a sacred hidden river my life-force flows in the gorge of the spine. I enter a dim corridor through the door of the spiritual eye, and speed on until at last the river of my life flows into the ocean of Life and loses itself in bliss.

PARAMAHANSA YOGANANDA

Too late I loved you, O Beauty so ancient yet ever new! Too late I loved you! And, behold, you were within me, and I out of myself, and there I searched for you.

SAINT AUGUSTINE

Waking up this morning, I smile.
Twenty-four brand new hours are before me.
I vow to live fully in each moment
and to look at all beings with eyes of
  compassion.

THICH NHAT HANH

Now observe: if thou fixest thy thoughts concerning heaven, and
wouldst willingly conceive in thy mind what it is and where it is and
how it is, thou needst not to cast thy thoughts many thousand miles off,
for that place, that heaven [above in the sky], is not thy heaven.

And though indeed that is united with thy heaven as one body, and so
together is but the one body of God, yet thou art not become a creature
in that very place which is above many hundred thousand miles off,
but thou art in the heaven of this world, which contains also in it such
a Deep as is not of any human numbering.

The true heaven is everywhere, even in that very place where thou
standest and goest; and so when thy spirit presses through the astral and
the fleshly, and apprehends the inmost moving of God, then it is clearly
in heaven.

But that there is assuredly a pure glorious heaven in all the three mov-
ings aloft above the deep of this world, in which God's Being together
with that of the holy angels springs up very purely, brightly, beauteously,
and joyfully, is undeniable. And he is not born of God that denies it.

JAKOB BÖHME

Do not say that I'll depart tomorrow
because even today I still arrive.
Look deeply: I arrive in every second
to be a bud on a spring branch,
to be a tiny bird, with wings still fragile,
     learning to sing in my new nest,
to be a caterpillar in the heart of flower,
to be a jewel hiding itself in a stone.
I still arrive, in order to laugh and to cry,
     in order to fear and to hope,
the rhythm of my heart is the birth and
     death of all that are alive.
I am the mayfly metamorphosing in the
     surface of the river,
and I am the bird which, when spring comes,
     arrives in time to eat the mayfly.
I am the frog swimming happily in the
     clear water of a pond,
and I am also the grass-snake who,
     approaching in silence,
     feeds itself on the frog.
I am the child in Uganda, all skin and bones,
     my legs as thin as bamboo sticks,
and I am the arms merchant, selling deadly
     weapons to Uganda.
I am the 12-year-old girl, refugee
     on a small boat,
who throws herself into the ocean after
     being raped by a sea pirate,
and I am the pirate, my heart not yet capable
     of seeing and loving.
I am a member of the politburo, with
     plenty of power in my hands,
and I am the man who has to pay his
     "debt of blood" to my people,

dying slowly in a forced labor camp.
My joy is like spring, so warm it makes
* flowers bloom in all walks of life.*
My pain is like a river of tears, so full it
* fills up the four oceans.*
Please call me by my true names,
so I can hear all my cries and my laughs at once,
so I can see that my joy and pain are one.
Please call me by my true names,
* so I can wake up,*
and so the door of my heart can be left open,
the door of compassion.

THICH NHAT HANH

In the still night by the vacant window,
wrapped in monk's robe I sit in meditation,
navel and nostrils lined up straight,
ears paired to the slope of shoulders.
Window whitens—the moon comes up;
rain's stopped, but drops go on dripping.
Wonderful—the mood of this moment—
distant, vast, known to me only!

RYOKAN

I will give up thinking of others.
If I want to think of others,
I think of my own Self within them.
I give up looking at others.
If I want to look at others,
I look at my own Self in them.
I look at my own Self
and become immersed in my own ecstasy.

SWAMI MUKTANANDA (ADAPTED)

Give heed, my child, lift your eyes,
behold the one who is standing here,
Behold, my child! Waiting now to fit
and set you here apart.
Give heed, my child, Look!
Sacred ointment now is here come to you.
Give heed, my child, lift your eyes,
behold the one who has holy made.
Behold, my child! You are set apart,
and finished is the task.
Give heed, my child. Look!
Sacred ointment now has set you apart.

PAWNEE SONG

PRAYERS FOR THE CREATIVE SPIRIT

There then was neither Aught nor Nought,
No air nor sky beyond.
What covered all? Where rested all?
In watery gulf profound?
Nor death was there, nor deathlessness,
Nor change of night and day.
That One breathed calmly, self-sustained:
Nor else beyond It lay.
Gloom hid in gloom existed first—
One sea eluding view.
That One, a void in chaos wrapt,
By inward fervor grew.
Within It first arose desire,
The primal germ of mind,
Which nothing with existence links,
As sages searching find.
The kindling ray that shot across
The dark and drear abyss,—
Was it beneath? Or high aloft?
What bard can answer this?
There fecundating powers were found,
and mighty forces strove,
A self-supporting mass beneath,
And energy above.
Who knows, whoe'er hath told, from whence
This vast creation rose?
No gods had then been born, who then can
e'er the truth disclose?
Whence sprang this world, and whether framed
By hand divine or no,
Its lord in heaven alone can tell,—
If even he can show.

THE RIG-VEDA, HYMN 129 (ANCIENT INDIA)

"One who has a man's wings
And a woman's also
Is in himself a womb of the world"
And, being a womb of the world,
Continuously, endlessly,
Gives birth;
One who, preferring light,
Prefers darkness also
Is in himself an image of the world
And, being an image of the world,
Is continuously, endlessly
The dwelling of creation.

LAO-TZU

But by what means did you make heaven and earth? What tool did you
use for this vast work? You did not work as a human craftsman does,
making one thing out of something else as his mind directs. His mind
can impose upon his material whatever form it perceives within itself
by its inner eye. But how could his mind do this unless it was because
you had made it?

SAINT AUGUSTINE

Patch the wind in the pines
To your hempen robes;
Use the moon as a pillow,
The ocean waves as your sheet.
Men are perplexed
When asked what Buddha is;
No one knows
It is his own mind.
Those who seek the Dharma
In the depths,
Are those who leave it
Behind in the shallows.

SHIDO MUNAN

God's wisdom in manifesting the world . . . is that which was known
should come forth visibly. Until He made visible that which He knew,
He did not impose upon the world the pains and throes of delivery. Not
for a single moment can you sit inactive, without some evil or goodness
issuing from you. These cravings for action were committed to you so
that your secret heart might become visible. How should the reel, the
body, ever be at rest seeing that the end of the thread, the mind, is
always tugging it? The token of that tugging is your restless; to be inac-
tive is for you like the agony of death. This world and the world beyond
are forever giving birth; every cause is a mother, whereof the effect is the
child. As soon as the effect is born it becomes a cause, so that other mar-
velous effects may be born of it. These causes mount back generation on
generation, but it requires a very illumined eye to see the links.

JALAL AL-DIN RUMI

You've hidden me, O Jesus, in Your face . . .
My God and Friend! Oh, hear me as I sing
Of what is inexpressible the grace
Of carrying the Cross . . . of suffering.
For long I've drunk a draught of tears, like You,
I've shared Your cup of sorrows: yet in this
That suffering has charms my heart knows, too;
One can save sinners—through the Cross, this is!

SAINT THERESE OF LISIEUX

Life is mostly froth and bubble,
Two things stand like stone,
Kindness in another's trouble,
Courage in your own.

ADAM LINDSAY GORDON

PRAYERS OF PRAISE

*God is One and alone, and none other exists with Him; God is the
One, the One who has made all things.*

*He is eternal and infinite; He has endured for countless ages, and He
shall endure to all eternity.*

God is a spirit, a hidden spirit, the Spirit of spirits, the Divine Spirit.

*He is a mystery to His creatures, and no man knows how to know Him.
His names are innumerable; they are manifold, and no one knows their
number.*

*God has made the universe, and He has created all that is in it; He has
stretched out the heavens and founded the earth. What His heart conceived came to pass straightway, and when He had spoken His word
came to pass, and it shall endure forever.*

THE EGYPTIAN BOOK OF THE DEAD

*For I remember the kind of man I was, O Lord, and it is a sweet task
to confess how you tamed me by pricking my heart with your goad; how
you bridged every valley, leveled every mountain and hill of my
thoughts; how you cut straight through their windings, paved their
rough paths . . .*

SAINT AUGUSTINE

To every thing there is a season, and a time to every purpose under the heaven:

A time to be born, and a time to die; a time to plant, and a time to pluck up that which is planted;

A time to kill, and a time to heal; a time to break down, and a time to build up;

A time to weep, and a time to laugh; a time to mourn, and a time to dance;

A time to cast away stones, and a time to gather stones together; a time to embrace, and a time to refrain from embracing;

A time to get, and a time to lose; a time to keep, and a time to cast away;

A time to rend, and a time to sew; a time to keep silence, and a time to speak;

A time to love, and a time to hate; a time of war, and a time of peace.

What profit hath he that worketh in that wherein he laboreth?

I have seen the travail, which God hath given to the sons of men to be exercised in it.

He hath made every thing beautiful in his time: also he hath set the world in their heart, so that no man can find out the work that God maketh from the beginning to the end.

I know that there is no good in them, but for a man to rejoice, and to do good in this life.

And also that every man should eat and drink, and enjoy the good of all his labor, it is the gift of God.

I know that, whatsoever God doeth, it shall be for ever: nothing can be put to it, nor any thing taken from it; and God doeth it, that men should fear before him.

That which hath been is now; and that which is to be hath already been; and God requireth that which is past.

And moreover I saw under the sun the place of judgment, that wickedness was there; and the place of righteousness, that iniquity was there.

I said in mine heart, God shall judge the righteous and the wicked; for there is a time for every purpose and for every work.

*I said in mine heart concerning the estate of the sons of men, that God
  might manifest them, and that they might see that they themselves
  are beasts.*

*For that which befalleth the sons of men befalleth beasts; even one thing
  befalleth them: as the one dieth, so dieth the other; yea, they have all
  one breath; so that a man hath no preeminence above a beast; for all
  is vanity.*

All go unto one place; all are of the dust, and all turn to dust again.

*Who knoweth the spirit of man that goeth upward, and the spirit of the
  beast that goeth downward to the earth?*

*Wherefore I perceive that there is nothing better, than that a man
  should rejoice in his own works; that that is his portion: for who
  shall bring him to see what shall be after him?*

ECCLESIASTES 3

*To thee, O Master that lovest men, I hasten on rising from sleep; by thy
mercy I go forth to do thy work, and I pray to thee: help me at all times,
in everything; deliver me from every evil thing of this world and from
every attach of the devil; save me and bring me to thine eternal
kingdom. For thou art my Creator, the Giver and Provider of
everything good; in thee is all my hope, and to thee I ascribe glory, now
and ever, and to the ages of ages. Amen.*

SAINT MACARIUS

For each new morning with its light,
For rest and shelter of the night,
For health and food, for love and friends,
For everything thy goodness sends.

RALPH WALDO EMERSON

Praise, my soul, the King of Heaven,
To His feet thy tribute bring;
Ransom'd heal'd, restored, forgiven,
Evermore His praises sing;
Alleluia! Alleluia!
Praise the everlasting King.
Praise Him for His grace and favor
To our fathers in distress;
Praise Him still the same as ever,
Slow to chide, and swift to bless;
Alleluia! Alleluia!
Glorious in His faithfulness.
Father-like, He tends and spares us,
Well our feeble frame He knows;
In His hands He gently bears us,
Rescues us from all our foes;
Alleluia! Alleluia!
Widely yet His mercy flows.
Angels in the height, adore Him;
Ye behold Him face to face;
Saints triumphant, bow before Him, gathers in from every race;
Alleluia! Alleluia!
Praise with us the God of grace.

H. F. LYTE

PRAYERS FOR CALM

There is no permanence.
Do we build a house to stand for ever, do we seal a contract to hold for
   all time?
Do brothers divide an inheritance to keep for ever, does the flood-time
   of rivers endure? . . . From the days of old there is no permanence.
The sleeping and the dead, how alike they are, they are like a painted
   death.
What is there between the master and the servant when both have ful
   filled their doom? When the Anunnaki, the judges [of the dead],
   come together, and Mammetun the mother of destinies, together
   they decree the fates of men.
Life and death they allot but the day of death they do not disclose.
                    ANONYMOUS BABYLONIAN

Never the spirit was born; the spirit shall cease to be never;
Never was time it was not; End and Beginning are dreams!
Birthless and deathless and changeless remaineth the spirit for ever.
                    THE BHAGAVAD GITA

Time, like a brilliant steed with seven rays,
And with a thousand eyes, imperishable,
Full of fecundity, bears all things onward.
On him ascend the learned and the wise.
Time, like a seven-wheeled, seven-naved car, moves on.
His rolling wheels are all the worlds, his axle
Is immortality. He is the first of gods.
We see him like an overflowing jar;
We see him multiplied in various forms.
He draws forth and encompasses the worlds;
He is all future worlds; he is their father;
He is their son; there is no power like him.
The past and future issue out of Time,
All sacred knowledge and austerity.
From Time the earth and waters were produced;
From Time, the rising, setting, burning sun;
From Time, the wind;
Through Time the earth is vast;
Through Time the eye perceives; mind, breath, and name
in him are comprehended.
All rejoice
When Time arrives—the monarch who has conquered
This world, the highest world, the holy worlds,
Yea, all the worlds—and ever marches on.

ARTHAVA VEDA, BOOK 19, HYMN 59

Be merciful unto me, O God, be merciful unto me: for my soul trusteth
in thee: yea, in the shadow of thy wings will I make my refuge, until
these calamities be overpast.

PSALM 57:1

Slow me down, Lord!
Ease the pounding of my heart
By the quieting of my mind.
Steady my harried pace
With a vision of the eternal reach of time.
Give me,
Amidst the confusions of my day,
The calmness of the everlasting hills.
Break the tensions of my nerves
With the soothing music of the singing streams
That live in my memory.
Help me to know
The magical power of sleep.
Teach me the art
Of taking minute vacations of slowing down
to look at a flower;
to chat with an old friend or make a new one;
to pat a stray dog;
to watch a spider build a web;
to smile at a child;
or to read a few lines from a good book.
Remind me each day
That the race is not always to the swift;
That there is more to life than increasing its speed.
Let me look upward
Into the branches of the towering oak
And know that it grew great and strong
Because it grew slowly and well.
Slow me down, Lord,
And inspire me to send my roots deep
Into the soil of life's enduring values
That I may grow toward the stars
Of my greater destiny.

WILFRED A. PETERSON

Darkness and light divide the tall sky,
the rumble of thunder passes over distant mountains.
The evening is cool, and beyond the slackening rain,
through broken clouds, a moon immaculate.

ISHIKAWA JOZAN

May there always be work for your hands to do
May your purse always hold a coin or two
May the sun always shine upon your window pane
May a rainbow be certain to follow each rain
May the hand of a friend always be near to you and
May God fill your heart with gladness to cheer you.

IRISH

Where there is charity and wisdom,
there is neither fear nor ignorance.
Where there is patience and humility,
there is neither anger nor vexation.
Where there is poverty and joy,
there is neither greed nor avarice.
Where there is peace and meditation,
there is neither anxiety nor doubt.

SAINT FRANCIS OF ASSISI

Peace within, peace without,
Peace between two thoughts,
Peace between two individuals,
Peace between Heaven and earth.

SRI CHINMOY

PRAYERS FOR EVIL, ANGER, AND PAIN

I am a thousand times more evil
than anything you know of evil:
in this no one knows me
as I know myself.
Outwardly I am evil,
but inwardly I am even more so.
God and I, we know
my exterior and my interior.
Satan may be my guide
in the occasional venial sin;
but in a hundred deadly sins
I show Satan the way.

JĀMĪ

If Thou sendest evil upon us, it is in love. All the evils of the physical
world are intended for the good of Thy creatures, or are the
unavoidable attendants on that good. And Thou turnest that evil into
good. Thou visitest men with evil to bring them to repentance, to
increase their virtue to gain for them greater good hereafter. Nothing is
done in vain, but has its gracious end. Thou dost punish, yet in wrath
Thou dost remember mercy.

JOHN HENRY NEWMAN

In the name of God, the Compassionate, the Merciful;
Praise be to God, the Lord of the Worlds,
The Compassionate, the Merciful,
King of Judgment-day!
You alone do we worship, and to You alone do we turn for help.
Guide us in the straight Path;
The Path of those whom You have favored;
not of those with whom You are angered; nor of those who go astray.

ISLAMIC

God in heaven, you have helped my life to grow like a tree. Now something has happened. Satan, like a bird, has carried in one twig of his own choosing after another. Before I knew it he had built a dwelling place and was living in it. Tonight, my Father, I am throwing out both the bird and the nest.

NIGERIAN

Why do you scorn others?
Can it be that you are that proud?
No matter how accomplished you are,
There are people ahead of you and behind you.
All beings on the path,
All victims of the same existence,
All with body, mind, and spirit.
No one is better than the next person.
Help others for all the times that you have been ignored.
Be kind to others for all the times that you have been scorned.

DENG MING-DAO

PRAYERS FOR JOY

Happy are the staffless
They stumble not.
Happy are the homeless,
They are at home.
The stumblers only—like ourselves,
Need walk with staffs.
The home-chained only—like ourselves,
Must have a home.

MIKHAIL NAIMY

Be not perplexed,
Be not afraid
Everything passes
God does not change
Patience wins all things
He who has God lacks nothing
God alone suffices

TERESA OF AVILA

For in and out, above, about, below,
'Tis nothing but a Magic Shadow-show
Play'd in a Box whose Candle is the Sun,
Round which we Phantom Figures come and go.

OMAR KHAYYÁM

Dance, my heart! Dance today with joy.
The strains of love fill the days and the nights with music, and the
world is listening to its melodies:
Mad with joy, life and death dance to the rhythm of this music. The
hills and the sea and the earth dance.
The world of man dances in laughter and tears.
Why put on the robe of the monk, and live aloof from the world in
lonely pride?
Behold! My heart dances in the delight of a hundred arts; and the Cre
ator is well pleased.

KABIR

While life is yours, live joyously;
None can escape Death's searching eye:
When once this frame of ours they burn,
How shall it e'er again return?

THE CHÁRVÁKA

Let peace abound in our small company. Purge out of every heart the
lurking grudge. Give us grace and strength to forbear and to persevere.
Offenders ourselves, give us the grace to accept and to forgive offenders.
Forgetful, help us to bear cheerfully the forgetfulness of others. Give us
courage and gaiety and the quiet mind.

CHRISTIAN

All shall be Amen and Alleluia.
We shall rest and we shall see.
We shall see and we shall know.
We shall know and we shall love.
We shall love and we shall praise.
Behold our end which is no end.

SAINT AUGUSTINE

Cheer up, cheer up, cheer up . . .
Cheer up, don't be concerned.
Look at the world.
The world is pretty.
You my patron Mother, Mother Conception . . .
My little Virgin doll, Holy Rosary, Mother Mazatlan
My father Holy Rosary,
Woman of the whirlpool in the lake am I, woman who waits am I,
Woman who tries am I, clean woman am I,
Oh Jesus, my patron Mother, look at this world.
Look how it is, dangerous world, dark world,
I'm going to free this the mushroom says, I'm going to dry it out in the
*   sunlight,*
the mushroom says,
Woman of the hunting dog am I,
My patron Mother, Mother Conception
My Virgin Magdalene, Mother Conception . . .

MARIA SABINA (SHAMANIC)

Sitting at the edge of the lake, I thought to myself, "This great loving gift has come to me.
Let me lovingly drink it."

EKNATH

God tells me that
Only a perfection-heart-voice
Is entitled to
A satisfaction-happiness-choice.

SRI CHINMOY

If you want to choose happiness
In life,
Then choose willingness first.
Happiness will automatically follow.

SRI CHINMOY

The Self is the light of all lights,
it is the breath of the breaths,
it is the eye of the eyes,
it is the fragrance of all other fragrances,
and also it is the happiness
that I experience in myself.

SWAMI MUKTANANDA (ADAPTED)

DEVOTIONAL PRAYERS

In the name of God, the merciful, the compassionate.

O Thou who nurturest the mind, who adornest the body.

O Thou who givest wisdom, who showest mercy on the foolish, Creator and Sustainer of Earth and time, Guardian and Defender of dweller and dwelling: dwelling and dweller, all is of thy creation; time and earth, all under the control of thy omnipotence, O Thou the Ineffable.

HAKIM ABU' L-MAJD MAJDUD SANAI OF GHAZNA

Lord, you are my lover,
My longing,
My flowing stream,
My sun,
And I am your reflection.

MECHTILD OF MAGDEBURG

The Lord is my shepherd; I shall not want.

He maketh me to lie down in green pastures: he leadeth me beside still waters.

He restoreth my soul: he leadeth me in the paths of righteousness for his name's sake.

Yea, though I walk through the valley of the shadow of death, I will fear no evil: for thou art with me; thy rod and thy staff they comfort me.

Thou preparest a table before me in the presence of mine enemies: thou anointest my head with oil, my cup runneth over.

Surely goodness and mercy shall follow me all the days of my life: and I will dwell in the house of the Lord for ever.

PSALM 23

The heavens declare the glory of God,
The skies proclaim His handiwork.
Day unto day utters a message,
Night unto night reveals knowledge.
There is no speech, there are no words,
Neither is their voice heard.
Yet their eloquence resounds throughout all the earth,
And their testimony to the end of the world.
A tent in the heavens has He set for the sun,
Which goes forth as a bridegroom from his chamber,
And rejoices as a hero to run his course.
From one end of the heaven it goes forth;
It moves round to the ends of it, missing nothing with its heat.

PSALM 19:1–6

Hail to thee, mighty Lord, all-potent Vishnu!
Soul of the universe, unchangeable,
Holy, eternal, always one in nature,
Whether revealed as Brahma, Hari, Siva—
Creator or Preserver or Destroyer—
Thou art the cause of final liberation;
Whose form is one, yet manifold; whose essence
Is one, yet diverse; tenuous, yet vast;
Discernible, yet indiscernible;
Root of the world, yet of the world composed;
Prop of the universe, yet more minute
Than earth's minutest particles; abiding
In every creature, yet without defilement,
Imperishable, one with perfect wisdom.

VISHNU PURANA

Waiting the word of the Master,
Watching the Hidden Light;
Listening to catch His orders
In the very midst of the fight;
Seeing His slightest signal
Across the heads of the throng;
Hearing His faintest whisper
Above Earth's loudest song.

ALCYONE (J. KRISHNAMURTI)

Blessed are the poor in spirit: for theirs is the kingdom of heaven.
Blessed are they that mourn: for they shall be comforted.
Blessed are the meek: for they shall inherit the earth.
Blessed are they which do hunger and thirst after righteousness: for they
*   shall be filled.*
Blessed are the merciful: for they shall obtain mercy.
Blessed are the pure in heart: for they shall see God.
Blessed are the peacemakers: for they shall be called the children of God.

MATTHEW 5:3–9

God be in my head,
And in my understanding;
God be in my eyes,
And in my looking;
God be in my mouth,
And in my speaking;
God be in my heart,
And in my thinking;
God be at my end,
And at my departing.

ANONYMOUS

Our Father who art in heaven,
Hallowed be Thy name,
Thy kingdom come,
Thy will be done,
On earth, as it is in heaven.
Give us our daily bread,
And forgive us our trespasses,
As we forgive them who trespass against us.
And lead us not into temptation,
But deliver us from evil;
For thine is the kingdom,
And the power,
And the glory,
Forever and ever,
Amen.

                                    MATTHEW 6:9–13

So God, you are the one who comes after.
It is sons who inherit,
while fathers die.
Sons stand and bloom,
You are my heir.

                                    RILKE

Because he hath set his love upon me, therefore will I deliver him:
I will set him on high, because he hath known my name.
He shall call upon me and I will answer him:
I will be with him in trouble:
I will deliver him, and honor him.

                                    PSALM 91:14–15

Soul of Christ, sanctify me,
Body of Christ, save me,
Blood of Christ, refresh me,
Water from the side of Christ, wash me,
Passion of Christ, strengthen me,
O good Jesus, hear me,
Within your wounds hide me,
Let me never be separated from you,
From the powers of darkness defend me,
In the hour of my death call me,
And bid me come to you,
That with your saints I may praise you
For ever and ever. Amen.

ANIMA CHRISTI

Holy Spirit, Spirit of the Living God,
you breathe in us
on all that is inadequate and fragile,
You make living water spring even
from our hurts themselves.
And through you, the valley of tears
becomes a place of wellsprings.
So, in an inner life
with neither beginning nor end,
your continual presence
makes new freshness break through. Amen.

BROTHER ROGER OF TAIZÉ

PRAYERS FOR HEALTH

*O let us live in joy, in love amongst those who hate! Among men who
hate, let us live in love.*

*O let us live in joy, in health amongst those who are ill! Among men
who are ill, let us live in health.*

THE DHAMMAPADA (INDIA)

*There is a balm in Gilead to make the wounded whole;
There is a balm in Gilead to heal the sin-sick soul.
Sometimes I feel discouraged,
And think my work's in vain,
But then the Holy Spirit
revives my soul again.
If you can't preach like Peter,
If you can't pray like Paul,
Just tell the love of Jesus,
And say he died for all.*

AFRICAN-AMERICAN

*Your pain is the breaking of the shell that encloses your understanding.
Even as the stone of the fruit must break, that its heart may stand in
    the sun,
so must you know pain.
And could you keep your heart in wonder at the daily miracles of your
    life,
your pain would not seem less wondrous than your joy;
And you would accept the seasons of your heart, even as you have
    always accepted the seasons that pass over your fields.
And you would watch with serenity through the winters of your grief.*

KAHLIL GIBRAN

In the house made of dawn.
In the story made of dawn.
On the trail of dawn.
O, Talking God.
His feet, my feet, restore.
His limbs, my limbs, restore.
His body, my body, restore.
His mind, my mind, restore.
His voice, my voice, restore.
His plumes, my plumes, restore.
With beauty before him, with beauty before me.
With beauty behind him, with beauty behind me.
With beauty above him, with beauty above me.
With beauty below him, with beauty below me.
With beauty around him, with beauty around me.
With pollen beautiful in his voice, with pollen beautiful in my voice.
It is finished in beauty.
It is finished in beauty.
In the house of evening light.
From the story made of evening light.
On the trail of evening light.

NAVAJO

But what avail the largest gifts of Heaven,
When drooping health and spirits go amiss?
How tasteless then whatever can be given!
Health is the vital principle of bliss.

JAMES THOMSON

We bow mind and heart in prayer before God. . . . We silence the outer self and banish worldly matters and thoughts. With deep and compassionate love for all mankind we await the incoming of the Spirit. . . . Spiritual power now encompasses us. Steadily, quietly, deeply, we breathe in the Spirit of God. . . . We pray: Fill us, O Spirit—fill us— fill us—and bless our endeavor to heal.

Being thus attuned, and steadfast in the light of God and the power of God's angels, we remember all those who are sick and who suffer. . . . We especially concentrate upon (here speak the name of the patient).

We hold him or her in a ray of spiritual light. We concentrate and project healing power to (here speak the name of the patient).

We behold him or her as helped, as healed, as made perfect in God. . . .

We thank thee Lord for thy presence, and the blessing of thy healing grace on these thy children.

WHITE EAGLE

LIFE-AFFIRMING PRAYERS

New every morning is the love
Our wakening and uprising prove;
Through sleep and darkness safely brought,
Restored to life, and power, and thought.
New mercies, each returning day,
Hover around us while we pray;
New perils past, new sins forgiven,
New thoughts of God, new hopes of Heaven.
If on our daily course our mind
Be set to hallow all we find,
New treasures still, of countless price,
God will provide for sacrifice.
The trivial round, the common task,
Will furnish all we need to ask,
Room to deny ourselves, a road
To bring us daily nearer God.
Only, O Lord, in Thy dear love
Fit us for perfect rest above;
And help us, this and every day,
To live more nearly as we pray.

KEBLE

You who are the true sun of the world, rising
and never going down, who by your most
wholesome appearing and sight nourishes and
makes joyful all things in heaven as on earth; we
bessech you mercifully and favorably to shine in
our hearts, that the night and darkness of sin,
and the mists of error on every side being driven
away, and with you shining in our hearts, we
may all our life long ago without any stumbling
or offense, and may walk as in the daytime,
being pure and clean from the works of
darkness, and abounding in all good works
which you have prepared for us to walk in.

DESIDERIUS ERASMUS

The source of being is above,
which gives life to all people;
For people are satisfied, and do not die of famine,
For the Lord gives them life,
that they may live prosperously
on the earth and not die of famine.

ZULU (SOUTH AFRICA)

I would be true for there are those who trust me,
I would be pure for there are those who care,
I would be strong for there is much to suffer,
I would be brave for there is much to dare,
I would be friend of all, the foe, the friendless
I would be giving and forget the gift
I would be humble for I know my weakness
I would look up, and laugh, and love, and live.

ANONYMOUS

A thing of beauty is a joy for ever;
Its loveliness increases; it will never
Pass into nothingness; but still will keep
A bower quiet for us, and a sleep
Full of sweet dreams, and health,
and quiet breathing.

JOHN KEATS

Whenever there is a withering of the Law and an uprising of
lawlessness on all sides, then I manifest Myself. For the salvation of the
righteous and the destruction of such as do evil, I come to birth age
after age.

THE BHAGAVAD GITA

Woman saint am I, he says, spirit woman am I, he says,
Illuminated woman am I, he says, yes Jesus says,
I am going to burn the world, he says, yes Jesus Christ says,
Woman who examines am I,
No one frightens me, he says,
No one is two-faced to me, he says,
I'm not surprised, he says, I'm not frightened, he says,
I give account to the judge, he says, I give account to the government, he
*   says,*
And I give account to my bishop, he says,
The good, clean bishop, he says, the good clean nun, he says,
Yes Jesus Christ says, yes Jesus says,
Yes Jesus says, yes Jesus Christ says,
I throw about, I scatter, he says,
Yes Jesus Christ says, yes I am going to spread out in the main trail, he
*   says,*
Only ounces, only pounds, he says, yes Jesus Christ says,
Woman who thus was born no less am I, he says, woman who thus
*   came into the world no less am I, he says,*
. . . clock woman am I, he says,
Yes, Jesus says, I am going to burn the world, he says. . . .

                              MARIA SABINA (SHAMANIC)

Even as all waters flow into the ocean, but the ocean never overflows,
*   even so the sage feels desires, but he is ever one in his infinite peace.*
Humility, unostentatiousness, non-injuring,
Forgiveness, simplicity, purity, steadfastness,
Self-control; this is declared to be wisdom;
What is opposed to this is ignorance.

                              THE BHAGAVAD GITA

The wise, who knows That One hidden
in the cave of the heart, is liberated
From the fetters of joy and sorrow.
A mortal having realized through discrimination the subtle-Self (Immortal Spirit)
rejoices, because he has obtained that which is the Source of all joy.

THE UPANISHADS

Honor Him, Honor Him
The revealed God.
I am still young,
An inexperienced fool,
But day by day
I strive aloft toward wisdom's light.
Help me to bear the burden,
Show me life's revelation.

CHINESE SACRIFICIAL ODE

If thou art powerful, respect knowledge and calmness of language.
Command only to direct; to be absolute is to run into evil. Let not thy
heart be haughty, neither let it be mean. Do not let thy orders remain
unsaid and cause thy answers to penetrate; but speak without heat,
assume a serious countenance. As for the vivacity of an ardent heart,
temper it; the gentle man penetrates all obstacles. He who agitates
himself all the day long has not a good moment; and he who amuses
himself all the day long keeps not his fortune.

PTAH-HOTEP

Lord of the Mountain,
Reared within the Mountain
Young Man, Chieftain,
Here's a young man's prayer!
Hear a prayer for cleanness.
Keeper of the strong rain,
Drumming on the mountain;
Lord of the small rain
That restores the earth in newness;
Keeper of the clean rain,
Hear a prayer for wholeness,
Young Man, Chieftain,
Hear a prayer for fleetness.
Keeper of the deer's way,
Reared among the eagles,
Clear my feet of slothness.
Hear a prayer for courage.
Lord of the thin peaks,
Reared amid the thunder;
Keeper of the headlands
Holding up the harvest,
Keeper of the strong rocks
Hear a prayer for staunchness.
Young Man, Chieftain,
Spirit of the Mountain!

NAVAJO

When the wind blows
that is my medicine
When it rains
that is my medicine
When it hails
that is my medicine
When it becomes clear after a storm
that is my medicine

ANONYMOUS

My daily activities are not different,
Only I am naturally in harmony with them.
Taking nothing, renouncing nothing,
In every circumstance no hindrance, no conflict.
Drawing water, carrying firewood,
This is supernatural power, this the marvelous activity.

LAO-TZU

I will sing of well-founded Gaia, Mother of All, eldest of all beings, she
feeds all creatures that are in the world, all that go upon the goodly
land and all that are in the paths of the sea, and all that fly: these are
fed of her store.

HOMERIC HYMN

PRAYERS FOR THE DEAD OR DYING
AND THOSE WHO MOURN

I dream of a vase of humble and simple clay,
to keep your ashes near my watchful eyes;
and for you my cheek will be the wall of the vase
and my soul and your soul will be satisfied.
I will not sift them into a vase of burning gold,
not into a pagan urn that mimics carnal lines;
I want only a vase of simple clay to hold
you humbly like a fold in this skirt of mine.
One of these afternoons I'll gather clay
by the river, and I'll shape it with trembling hand.
Women, bearing sheaves, will pass my way,
not guessing I fashion a bed for a husband.
The fistful of dust, I hold in my hands,
will noiseless pour, like a thread of tears.
I will seal this vase with an infinite kiss,
and I'll cover you only with my endless gaze!

GABRIELA MISTRAL

I died a mineral and became a plant.
I died a plant and rose an animal.
I died an animal and I was a man.
Why should I fear? When was I less by dying?
Yet once more I shall die as man, to soar
With the blessed angels; but even from angelhood
I must pass on. All except God perishes.
When I have sacrificed my angel soul,
I shall become that which no mind ever conceived.
O, let me not exist! for Non-Existence proclaims,
"To Him we shall return."

JALAL AL-DIN RUMI

I planted the seed of holy words
in this world.
When long since the palm tree will have died,
the rock decayed;
When long since the shining monarchs
have been blown away like rotted leaves:
Through every deluge a thousand arks
will carry my word:
It will prevail!

SOURCE UNKNOWN BUT ATTRIBUTED TO "AN OLD SAGE"
IN WILHELM REICH, *LISTEN, LITTLE MAN!*

Almighty God, Father of all mercies and giver of all comfort: deal gra-
ciously, we pray thee, with those who mourn, that casting every care on
thee, they may know the consolation of thy love; through Jesus Christ
our Lord. Amen.

CHRISTIAN

O Father of all, we pray to thee for those whom we love, but see no
longer. Grant them thy peace; let light perpetual shine upon them; and
in thy loving wisdom and almighty power work in them the good pur-
pose of thy perfect will; through Jesus Christ our Lord. Amen.

CHRISTIAN

Bring us, O Lord God, at our last awakening into the house and gate
of heaven; to enter into that gate and dwell in that house, where there
shall be no darkness nor dazzling, but one equal light; no noise nor si-
lence, but one equal music, no fears nor hopes, but one equal possession;
no ends, nor beginnings, but one equal eternity; in the habitation of
thy glory and dominion, world without end. Amen.

JOHN DONNE

Promise me,
promise me this day
while the sun is just overhead
even as they strike you down
with a mountain of hate and violence,
remember, brother,
man is not our enemy.
Just your pity,
just your hate
invincible, limitless,
hatred will never let you face
the beast in man.
And one day, when you face this
beast alone, your courage intact,
your eyes kind,
out of your smile
will bloom a flower
and those who love you
will behold you
across 10,000 worlds of birth and dying.
Alone again
I'll go on with bent head
but knowing the immortality of love.
And on the long, rough road
both sun and moon will shine,
lighting my way.

THICH NHAT HANH

*Thy tears are for those beyond tears; and are thy words words of
wisdom? The wise grieve not for those who live; and they grieve not for
those who die—for life and death shall pass away.*

*Because we all have been for all time: I, and thou, and those kings of
men. And we shall be for all time, we all for ever and ever.*

*As the spirit of our mortal body wanders on in childhood, and youth
and old age, the Spirit wanders on to a new body: of this the sage has
no doubts.*

THE BHAGAVAD GITA

*Leaning on a cane by the wooded village,
trees rising thick all around:
a dog barks in the wake of a beggar;
in front of the farmer, the ox plowing.
A whole lifetime of cold stream waters,
in age and sickness, the evening sun sky—
I have tasted every pleasure of mist and sunset
in these ten-years-short-of-a-hundred.*

ISHIKAWA JOZAN

*I am that supreme and fiery force that sends forth all living sparks.
Death hath no part in me, yet I bestow death, wherefore I am girt
about with wisdom as with wings. I am that living and fiery essence of
the divine substance that glows in the beauty of the fields, and in the
shining water, and in the burning sun and the moon and the stars, and
in the force of the invisible wind, the breath of all living things, I
breathe in the green grass and in the flowers, and in the living waters.... All these live and do not die because I am in them.... I am
the source of the thundered word by which all creatures were made, I
permeate all things that they may not die. I am life.*

HILDEGARDE VON BINGEN

If you would indeed behold the spirit
of death, open your heart wide
unto the body of life.
For life and death are one, even as the
river and the sea are one.

KAHLIL GIBRAN

Out of life comes death,
and out of death, life,
Out of the young, the old,
and out of the old, the young,
Out of waking, sleep,
and out of sleep, waking,
the stream of creation and dissolution
never stop.

HERACLEITUS

Do not stray from the path of life and so court death; do not draw dis-
aster on yourselves by your own actions. For God did not make death,
and takes no pleasure in the destruction of any living thing; he created
all things that they might have being. The creative forces of the world
make for life; there is no deadly poison in them. Death is not king on
earth, for justice is immortal.

THE WISDOM OF SOLOMON (OLD TESTAMENT TEXTS NOT
INCLUDED IN THE BIBLE), THE APOCRYPHA

PRAYERS FOR ABUNDANCE

Grant that this year abundant harvest reign,
And be our granaries piled with rice and grain.
Let sheaves in myriads and in millions fill
Our barns. From these sweet wine we will distill,
To pour as solemn offerings at the shrine
Of those, who, passed away, are now divine;
The sainted sires and mothers of our line.
Pleased with such sacrifice may they bestow
Unnumbered blessings on the folk below.

ANONYMOUS (CHINESE CHOU DYNASTY B.C.E.), *THE SHIH CHING*, HYMN FOR THE HARVEST

May the kingdom of justice prevail!
May the believers be united in love!
May the hearts of the believers
be humble, high their wisdom,
and may they be guided in their
wisdom by the Lord.
O Hkalsa, say "Wahiguru,
Glory be to God!"
Entrust unto the Lord what thou
wishest to be accomplished.
The Lord will bring all matters
to fulfilment:
Know this as truth
evidenced by Himself.

SIKH

O Lord, O God,
creator of our land,
our earth, the trees,
the animals and humans,
all is for your honor.
The drums beat it out,
and people sing about it,
and they dance with noisy joy
that you are the Lord.
You also have pulled the other continents out of the sea.
What a wonderful world you have made out of the wet mud,
and what beautiful men and women!
We thank you for the beauty of this earth.
The grace of your creation is like a cool day between rainy seasons.
We drink in your creation with our eyes.
We listen to the birds' jubilee with our ears.
How strong and good and sure your earth smells,
and everything that grows there.
The sky above us is like a warm, soft Kente cloth,
because you are behind it,
else it would be cold and rough and uncomfortable.
We drink in your creation and cannot get enough of it.
But in doing this we forget the evil we have done.
Lord, we call you, we beg you:
tear us away from our sins and our death.
This wonderful world fades away.
And one day our eyes snap shut,
and all is over and dead that is not from you.
We are still slaves of the demons and the fetishes of this earth.
When we are not saved by you.
Bless us.
Bless our land and people.
Bless our forests with mahogany, wawa, and cacao.
Bless our fields with cassava and peanuts.
Bless the waters that flow through our land.

Fill them with fish and drive great schools of fish to our seacoast,
so that the fishermen in their unsteady boats
do not need to go out too far.
Be with us youth in our countries, and in all Africa,
and in the whole world.
Prepare us for the service that we should render.

ASHANTI (GHANA)

All my life lazy to try to get ahead,
I leave everything to the truth of Heaven.
In my sack three measures of rice,
by the stove one bundle of sticks—
why ask who's got satori, who hasn't?
What would I know about that dust, fame, and gain?
Rainy nights here in my thatched hut
I stick out my two legs any old way I please.

RYOKAN

I called for help, and there came to me a spirit of wisdom. I valued her above scepter and throne, and reckoned riches as nothing beside her; I counted no precious stone her equal, because all the gold in the world compared with her is but a little sand, and silver worth no more than clay. I loved her more than health and beauty; I preferred her to the light of day; for her radiance is unsleeping. So all good things together came to me with her, and in her hands was wealth past counting; and all was mine to enjoy, for all follows where wisdom leads, and I was in ignorance before, that she is the beginning of it all. What I learnt with pure intention I now share without grudging, nor do I hoard for myself the wealth that comes from her. She is an inexhaustible treasure for mankind, and those who profit by it become God's friends, commended to him by the gifts they derive from her instruction.

THE WISDOM OF SOLOMON (OLD TESTAMENT TEXTS NOT
INCLUDED IN THE BIBLE), THE APOCRYPHA

I spun some yarn to sell for food
And sold it for two silver coins.
I put a coin in each hand
Because I was afraid
That if I put both together in one hand
This great pile of wealth might hold me back.

RABI'A AL-ADAWIYYA

One day Rabi'a was sick,
And so her holy friends came to visit her, sent by her bedside,
And began putting down the world.
"You must be pretty interested in this 'world,'" said Rabi'a, "otherwise,
*   you wouldn't talk about it so much:*
Whoever breaks the merchandise
Has to have bought it first."

RABI'A AL-ADAWIYYA

In the creation of the heavens and the earth; in the alternation of night
and day; in the ships that sail the ocean with cargoes beneficial to man;
in the water which God sends down from the sky and with which He
revives the earth after its death, dispersing over it all manner of beasts;
in the disposal of the winds, and in the clouds that are driven between
sky and earth: surely in these there are signs for rational men.

THE QUR'AN

But I say to you, Love your enemies and pray for those who persecute
you, so that you may be sons of your Father who is in heaven; for he
makes his sun rise on the evil and on the good, and sends rain on the
just and on the unjust.

MATTHEW 5:44–45

Hear then, you Kings, take this to heart; learn your lesson, lords of the wide world; lend your ears, you rulers of the multitude, whose pride is in the myriads of your people. It is the Lord who gave you your authority; your power comes from the Most High.

THE WISDOM OF SOLOMON (OLD TESTAMENT TEXTS NOT
INCLUDED IN THE BIBLE), THE APOCRYPHA

Virtues are virtues because they give joy once they are practiced. If a virtue does not give joy, it is not a virtue.

HAZRAT INAYAT KHAN

Consideration is the greatest of all virtues, for in consideration all virtues are born. Veneration for God, courtesy toward others, respect of those who deserve it, kindness to those who are weak and feeble, sympathy with those who need it, all these come from consideration.

HAZRAT INAYAT KHAN

Were life's span extended to the four ages
And ten times more,
Were one known over the nine shores
Ever in humanity's fore,
Were one to achieve greatness
With a name noised over the earth,
If one found not favor with the Lord
What would it all be worth?

GURU NANAK

PRAYERS FOR LIGHT AND DARKNESS

Lighten our darkness, we beseech thee, O Lord; and by thy great mercy defend us from all perils and dangers of this night.

THE BOOK OF COMMON PRAYER

Almighty God, who art the light of the world, grant us Thy heavenly blessing. May the radiance of these lights, kindled in honor of this Festival, illumine our hearts, and brighten our home with the spirit of faith and love. Let the light of Thy Presence guide us, for in Thy light do we see light. Bless also with Thy spirit the homes of all Israel and all mankind, that happiness and peace may ever abide in them. Amen.

PRAYER FOR KINDLING THE LIGHTS

O Most High, help to bring thy light into the darkened conditions of the world! Be gracious to us thy humble servants and bless us with illumination as to that which is Divinely relevant to the fulfilment of thy will!

O Most High, inspire thy servants throughout the world to further efforts toward leading back thy children who are led astray to the right way, and to live and act on the faith of what has been taught by the great founders of the religions!

Bless all spiritual leaders with thy power and enable them to give help, joy, comfort, and reassurance to those suffering, to whom they minister!

SHINTO

All light is Thy radiance,
and shade is the shadow of Thy beauty.
Thou art both: in light as radiance,
in the dark as shade.
Thou changest Thy place,
but not Thyself, O light.
Light is Thy manifestation;
shade is Thy withdrawing.
In the light Thou art manifest;
in the shade Thou art hidden.
Light is Thine eye
and shade is its pupil.
The shade adds to the light
as zero adds to the figure.
Light represents Thy heavens
and shade Thy earth.

HAZRAT INAYAT KHAN

God is the light of the heavens and the earth; the likeness of his Light is
as a niche wherein is a lamp. The lamp is in a glass, the glass is as it
were a shining star, kindled from a blessed tree, an olive, neither of the
East nor of the West. Its oil would well-nigh shine, even if no fire
touched it. Light upon Light; God guides to His Light whom He will.
And God strikes similitudes for men, and God has knowledge of all
things.

ISLAMIC VERSE OF LIGHT

O Light of light, Thou art veiled to Thy creatures and they do not
attain to Thy light. O Light of light, Thy light illuminates the people of
heaven and enlightens the people of earth. O Light of all light, Thy
light is praised by all light.

ATTRIBUTED TO MUHAMMAD

By means of the Divine Lights the heart becomes polished so that it shines like a polished mirror. When it becomes a mirror one can see in it the reflection of all existing things and the reflection of the Kingdom and Majesty of God in His Realm then all the lights become one light and the chest becomes full with this shining light. He is like a man who observes his reflection in a mirror and sees in it at the same time the reflection of all that is before and behind him. Now when a ray of sun hits the mirror the whole house becomes flooded with light from the meeting of these two lights: the light of the sun-ray and the light of the mirror. Similarly the heart: when it is polished and shining it beholds the Realm of Divine Glory and the Divine Glory becomes revealed to it.

AL-HAKIM AT-TIRMIDHI

For now we see through a glass, darkly; but then face to face: now I know in part; but then shall I know even as also I am known.

I CORINTHIANS 13:12

We look not at the things which are seen, but at the things which are not seen: for the things which are seen are temporal; but the things which are not seen are eternal.

II CORINTHIANS 4:18

I, a stranger and afraid
In a world I never made.

ALFRED EDWARD HOUSMAN

This very world is a mansion of mirth; here I can eat, here drink and make merry.

SHRI RAMAKRISHNA

Whatever befalls the Earth befalls the sons of the Earth. Man does not weave the web of life, he is merely a strand in it. Whatever I do to the web I do to myself.

CHIEF SEATTLE (ADAPTED)

This love is not divine; it is mere greed
For flesh—an animal, instinctive need.
How long then will you seek for beauty here?
Seek the unseen, and beauty will appear.

FARID UD-DIN ATTAR

Whatever It was
That made this earth
the base,
the world its life,
the wind its pillar,
arranged the lotus and the moon,
and covered it all with folds
of sky,
with Itself inside,
To that Mystery
indifferent to differences,
to It I pray,
O Ramanatha.

DEVARA DASIMAYYA

PRAYERS FOR HEART AND SOUL

The world stands out on either side
No wider than the heart is wide;
Above the world is stretched the sky,
No higher than the soul is high.
The heart can push the sea and land
Farther away on either hand;
The soul can split the sky in two,
And let the face of God shine through.
But East and West will pinch the heart
That can not keep them pushed apart;
And he whose soul is flat—the sky
Will cave in on him by and by.

EDNA ST. VINCENT MILLAY

O God, the night has passed and the day has dawned. How I long to
know if Thou has accepted my prayers or if Thou has rejected them.
Therefore console me for it is Thine to console this state of mind. Thou
hast given me life and cared for me and Thine is the glory. If Thou
wantst to drive me from Thy door, yet I would not forsake it, for the
love that I bear in my heart toward Thee.

RABI'A AL-ADAWIYYA

I believe in the sun even when it is not shining.
I believe in love even when feeling it not.
I believe in God even when he is silent.

JEWISH

When washing your face, can you see your true self?
When urinating, can you remember true purity?
When eating, can you remember the cycles of all things?
When walking, can you feel the rotation of heaven?
When working, are you happy with what you do?
When speaking, are your words without guile?
When you shop, are you aware of your needs?
When you meet the suffering, do you help?
When confronted with death, are you unafraid and lucid?
When you meet conflict, do you work toward harmony?
When with your family, do you express benevolence?
When raising children, are you tender but firm?
When facing problems, are you far-seeing and tenacious?
When you are finished with work, do you take time to rest?
When preparing for rest, do you know how to settle your mind?
When sleeping, do you slip into absolute void?

DENG MING-DAO

If you are a king,
Will you have contentment?
If you are a beggar,
Will you have contentment?
Whatever your walk in life may be,
You will only have contentment through
Knowing yourself by yourself.

YOGASWAMI

Just to be is a blessing.
Just to live is holy.

RABBI ABRAHAM HESCHEL

Gradually the soul recognizes her beloved
and she rejoices once more,
yet weeping before him
as she remembers the disgrace of her former widowhood.
She adorns herself still more,
so that he might be pleased to stay with her.
He requires her to turn to face from her people
and the multitude of her adulterers
in whose midst she once was,
To devote herself only to her kind, her real Lord,
and to forget the house of the earthly father
where things went so badly with her
But to remember her Father who is in heaven.
And the prophet said in the Psalms:
"Hear, my daughter, and see, then incline your ear,
Forget your people and your father's house
for the King has desired your beauty; he is your Lord."

ANONYMOUS FOURTH-CENTURY GNOSTIC, *NAG HAMMADI*
GOSPELS, THE EXEGESIS OF THE SOUL

Holy Spirit
think through me
till your ideas
are my ideas

AMY CARMICHAEL

PRAYERS FOR WORK AND SUCCESS

May Shamash [the Sun God] give you your heart's desire, may he let you see with your eyes the thing accomplished which your lips have spoken; may he open a path for you where it is blocked, and a road for your feet to tread. May he open the mountains for your crossing, and may the night time bring you the blessings of night, and Lugulbanada, your guardian god, stand beside you for victory. May you have victory in the battle as though you fought with a child.

ANONYMOUS BABYLONIAN

The mighty sea, unmeasured mighty lake,
The fearsome home of multitudes of pearls—
As rivers, serving countless hosts of men,
Flow widely forth and to that ocean come:—
Just so, on him that giveth food, drink, clothes,
Who bed and seat and coverlet provides,
Torrents of merit flood that mortal wise,
As rivers, bearing water, reach the main.

SAMYUTTA NIKAYA

God, give us grace to accept with serenity the things that cannot be changed, courage to change the things which should be changed, and the wisdom to distinguish the one from the other.

REINHOLD NIEBUHR

Each morning I offer my body, my mind, and any ability that I possess, to be used by Thee, O Infinite Creator, in whatever way Thou dost choose to express Thyself through me. I know that all work is Thy work, and that no task is too difficult or too menial when offered to Thee in loving service.

PARAMAHANSA YOGANANDA

I shall say that I want it all.
If you ask me how much I want,
I shall tell you that I want it all.
You and I and everyone are flowing this morning
Into the marvelous stream of oneness.
Small pieces of imagination as we are,
We have come a long way to find ourselves,
And for ourselves in the dark,
The illusion of emancipation.
This morning my brother is back from his long adventure.
He kneels before the altar and his eyes are filled with tears.
His soul is looking for a shore to put an anchor,
My own image of long ago.
Let him cry his heart out.
Let him have his refuge for a thousand years.
Enough to dry all his tears.
Because one of these nights I shall come.
I have to come and set fire to this small cottage of his on a hill.
His last shelter.
My fire will destroy,
Destroy everything.
Taking away from him the only life raft he has, after a shipwreck.
In the utmost anguish of his soul,
The shell will break.
The light of the burning cottage,
Tears will run down my cheeks.
I shall be there to contemplate his new existence,
And hold his hands in mine,
And ask him how much he would want.
He will smile at me and say that he wants it all.
Just as I did.

THICH NHAT HANH

PRAYERS OF TRIBUTE

O my King,
I relish this loss of good name greatly.
Some will revile me, some will praise me,
But I shall follow my unfathomable path.
On this narrow path
I have met men of God.

MIRA BAI

O you who covers the high places with waters,
    who sets the sand as a bound to the sea and
upholds all things:
    the sun sings your praises, the moon gives
you glory,
    Every creature offers a hymn to you, his
author and creator forever.

EASTERN ORTHODOX

Oh God, Thou art more friend to me
than I am to myself.
I dedicate myself to Thee,
O Lord.

'ABDU'L-BAHÁ

It is Glory enough for me
That I should be Your servant.
It is grace enough for me
That You should be my Lord.

ARABIC

Recall that here on earth your happiness
   Lay in your looking after us! We pray
   That you who go on loving us, will bless
   Your children—will protect us still today.
You've reached your Homeland, where
      you're met and greeted by
Our mother dear—there, long
      before you, up on high:
  In heaven now you reign
  Together. Both again
     Watch over us!
  Recall Marie, that loving daughter who
  Was to your heart the dearest of us . . . yes,
  Recall, as well: she made life full for you
  With all her love and charm and happiness.
God called her then, so—for
     His sake!—you didn't cling:
Instead, you blessed the hand
     that offered Suffering.
  Your lovely "Diamond"—oh,
  The one that sparkled so,
    Remember now!
  And Pauline—she the "Pearl of Beauty"!—too:
  At home, a weak and timid "lamb"—but how
  God's strength has since possessed the one you knew;
  It's she who leads the flock of Carmel now!
Yes, she is Mother to
    your other children here—
Come, guide her here below,
    that one, to you so dear!
  Still, from your place above,
  Your little Carmel love! . . .
    Remember now . . .
  Your third child now recall, and all the prayer
  You offered up to God, so ardently . . .

He heard! She knows the earth and all that's there
    As exile for her spirit, Léonie
The Visitation hides
       her from the world, but she
Loves Jesus; and His peace
       now floods her like a sea!
  Recall, and hear the sighs—
  Her ardent longings—rise,
     Remember now!
  Recall, your faithful Céline also: she
  The angel who was taking care of you
  (For then God's gaze had meant that you would be
  Tried, by a choice so glorious—there too).
You reign in Heav'n . . . her task
     is finished. By her vow
Her life is given up
     to Jesus wholly now.
  Protect her, we entreat,
  The one you hear repeat,
    "Recall me now!"
  Remember, too, your "Little Queen": you know
  How lavish all her tendernesses were!
  Recall: her little footsteps faltered so—
  Your hand it was that always guided her.
Papa, you wished your child
     to keep her childhood: hence
You sought (for God alone)
     to guard her innocence . . .
  Her locks of gold—sight
  That gave you such delight—
    Recall them now!
  And often, too, up in the belvedere
  You'd take her on your knee, and you would bring
  Contentment to her with a prayer . . . she'd hear
  The gentle cradle-song that you would sing.

What she would see was Heav'n
     reflected in your face
When, there, your gaze was drawn
     profoundly into space.
  Song . . . of Eternity:
  The beauty there would be!—
    Recall that now.
  One Sunday—how that day was full of light—
  You pressed her to your heart, a father . . . you,
  In giving her a little flower of white,
  Agreed that she could fly to Carmel too!
Papa! Your love—which bore
     such heavy trials here—
Gave proof to her, by that,
     that it was most sincere!
  At Bayeux, and at Rome,
  You showed her Heav'n—her Home—
    Recall that now.
  Recall we saw the Holy Father's hand
  Rest on your forehead. Yet there was concealed
  One mystery! . . . you couldn't understand
  The print of God by which your brow was sealed.
Your children bless the cross,
     your bitter sorrow—how
You suffered then! But they
     are praying to you now.
  Your forehead bears a sign,
  In Heav'n! . . . in rays that shine,
    Nine lilies flower!!!

SAINT THERESE OF LISIEUX

PRAYERS FOR PURITY AND SIMPLICITY

O Lord, help me to be pure, but not yet.

SAINT AUGUSTINE

Grant me the ability to be alone;
may it be my custom to go outdoors each day
among the trees and grasses,
among all growing things,
and there may I be alone,
to talk with the one
that I belong to.

RABBI NACHMAN OF BRATZLAV

Where is Tao right now?
You say that it is all around me, but I
Only see my surroundings, only feel my own heartbeat.
Can you show me Tao without reasoning it out in my mind?
Can you help me see it here and now?
Can you help me feel it as doubtlessly as I touch?
You argue that Tao is beyond the senses,
But how do I know it exists?
You say that Tao is beyond definitions,
Then how will I understand it?
It is hard enough understanding the economy, my relationships,
The bewilderment of world events, violence, crime,
Drug abuse, political repression, and war,
With all these things requiring years to fathom,
How can I understand something that is
Colorless, nameless, flavorless, intangible, and silent?
Show me Tao! Show me Tao!

DENG MING-DAO

PRAYERS TO REASSURE

Grant us, O Lord, to pass this day in gladness
   and in peace
   without stumbling and without stain;
That, reaching the eventide
   victorious over all temptation,
We may praise you, the eternal God,
Who is blessed, and who governs all things,
World without end.

MOZARABIC LITURGY

God speaks to each of us as he makes us,
then walks with us silently out of the night.
These are the words we dimly hear:
You, sent out beyond your recall,
go to the limits of your longing.
Embody me.
Flare up like flame
and make big shadows I can move in.
Let everything happen to you: beauty and terror.
Just keep going. No feeling is final.
Don't let yourself lose me.
Nearby is the country they call life.
You will know it by its seriousness.
Give me your hand.

RILKE

Teach me to feel that I am enveloped always in the aureole of Thine all-protecting omnipresence, in birth, in sorrow, in joy, in activity, in meditation, in ignorance, in trials, in death, and in final emancipation.

Teach me to open the gate of meditation that alone leads to Thy blessed presence.

Behind the wave of my consciousness is the sea of cosmic consciousness. Under the ripple of my mind is the supporting ocean of Thy vastness. I am protected by Thy Divine Mind.

The light of goodness and Thy protective power are ever shining through me. I saw them not, because my eyes of wisdom were closed. Now Thy touch of peace has opened my eyes; Thy goodness and unfailing protection are flowing through me.

PARAMAHANSA YOGANANDA

In the cave of my heart dwells the Lord . . . who killed the Elephant-demon (which can destroy elephants), who destroyed the ferocious Tiger-demon (which can overcome even tigers), who has on him dead animals, and who has a white form (which has a majestic appearance). Whence is there fear for me!

SHANKARA (INDIA)

To reach satisfaction in all, desire its possession in nothing.
To come to possess all, desire the possession of nothing.
To arrive at being all, desire to be nothing.
To come to the knowledge of all, desire the knowledge of nothing.

JUAN DE LA CRUZ (JOHN OF THE CROSS)

Know with certain knowledge
that God does not grant any mortal
—no matter how great his strategy,
no matter how intense his seeking,
and no matter how powerful his machinations—
more than what is determined
in the Recollection of Wisdom.
And God does not withhold from any mortal,
on account of weakness or lack of wiles,
what it is determined shall come to him
according to the Recollection of Wisdom.
And the one who knows this
and acts on it
is the most comfortable of people
with the yield of what is useful,
while the one who rejects and doubts it
is the most troubled of people
with the detriment of what is harmful.
And many of the advantaged
are being lured into destruction
by advantages,
while many of the afflicted
are being affected constructively
by affliction.
So increase your gratefulness,
O hearer,
and reduce your haste,
and stay within the limitations
of your income.

HADRAT 'ALI

I am calling to you from afar;
Calling to you since the very beginning of days.
Calling to you across millennia,
For aeons of time—
Calling—calling. . . . Since always . . .
It is part of your being, my voice,
But it comes to you faintly and you only hear it sometimes;
"I don't know," you may say.
But somewhere you know.
"I can't hear," you say, "what is it and where?"
But somewhere you hear, and deep down you know.
For I am that in you which has been always;
I am that in you which will never end.
Even if you say, "Who is calling?"
Even if you think, "Who is that?"
Where will you run? Just tell me.
Can you run away from yourself?
For I am the Only One for you;
There is no other.
Your Promise, your Reward am I alone—
Your Punishment, your longing
And your Goal. . . .

                            ANONYMOUS

PRAYERS TO THE UNITY OF ALL LIFE

*There is no kind of beast on earth, nor fowl which flieth with its wings,
but the same is a people like unto you. Unto their Lord shall they
return. . . . God is the light of the heavens and of the earth.*

*Hast thou not seen how all in the heavens and in the earth uttereth the
praise of God?*

*The very birds as they spread their wings? Every creature knoweth its
prayer and its praise.*

THE QUR'AN

*Now under the loving kindness and care of the Buddha, each believer
of religion in the world transcends the differences of religion, race, and
nationality, discards small differences, and unites in oneness to discuss
sincerely how to annihilate strife from the earth, how to reconstruct a
world without arms, and how to build the welfare and peace of
mankind, so that never-ending light and happiness can be obtained for
the world of the future.*

BUDDHIST

*I lined them up side by side
That moment, events occurred
Four fruits, two flowers
Touch a tree, spin a web,
Turn a head, pay respect,
Sew, light, paint, blow.
Be me some.
Simple acts, hard to follow.*

PHILIP DUNN

May the winds, the oceans, the herbs, and night and days, the mother earth, the father heaven, all vegetation, the sun, be all sweet to us.

Let us follow the path of goodness for all times, like the sun and the moon moving eternally in the sky.

Let us be charitable to one another. Let us not kill or be violent with one another.

Let us know and appreciate the points of view of others. And let us unite.

May the God who is friendly, benevolent, all-encompassing, measurer of everything, the sovereign, the lord of speech, may He shower His blessings on us. . . .

Oh Lord, remove my indiscretion and arrogance; control my mind. Put an end to the snare of endless desires. Broaden the sphere of compassion and help me to cross the ocean of existence.

HINDU

God has created all things for good; all things for their greatest good; everything for its own good. What is the good of one is not the good of another; what makes one man happy would make another unhappy. God has determined, unless I interfere with His plan, that I should reach that which will be my greatest happiness. He looks on me individually, He calls me by my name, He knows what I can do, what I can best be, what is my greatest happiness, and He means to give it me.

God knows what is my greatest happiness, but I do not. There is no rule about what is happy and good; what suits one would not suit another. And the ways by which perfection is reached vary very much; the medicines necessary for our souls are very different from each other. Thus God leads us by strange ways; we know He wills our happiness, but we neither know what our happiness is, nor the way. We are blind; left to ourselves we should take the wrong way; we must leave it to Him.

JOHN HENRY NEWMAN

PRAYERS FOR PEACE AND SILENCE

Adorable Presence!
Thou who art within and without,
above and below and all around;
Thou who art interpenetrating
the very cells of our being—
Thou who art the Eye of our eyes,
the Ear of our ears,
the Heart of our hearts,
the Mind of our minds,
the Breath of our breaths,
the Life of our lives,
and the Soul of our souls.
Bless us Dear God,
to be aware of Thy Presence
Now and Here.
This is all that we ask of Thee;
May all be aware of Thy Presence in
the East and the West,
and the North and the South.
May Peace and Goodwill abide
among individuals as well as among
communities and nations.
This is our Earnest Prayer.
May Peace be unto All
Om Shanti! Peace! Shalom!

SWAMI OMKAR, PEACE PRAYER OFFERED BY THE MISSION
OF PEACE SHANTI ASHRAM, INDIA, FOR THE 1993 PARLIA-
MENT OF THE WORLD'S RELIGIONS (INDIA)

Oh God,
You are Peace.
From You comes Peace,
To You returns Peace.
Revive us with a salutation of Peace,
and lead us to your abode of Peace.

ISLAMIC

Lord, make me an instrument of thy peace.
Where there is hatred let me sow love;
Where there is injury, pardon;
Where there is doubt, faith;
Where there is despair, hope;
Where there is darkness, light;
Where there is sadness, joy.
O divine Master,
Grant that I may not so much seek to be consoled,
As to console;
Not so much to be understood,
As to understand;
Nor so much to be loved,
As to love.
For it is in giving that we receive.
It is in pardoning that we are pardoned.
It is in dying that we awaken to eternal life.

SAINT FRANCIS OF ASSISI

Let us know peace.
For as long as the moon shall rise,
For as long as the rivers shall flow,
For as long as the sun shall shine,
For as long as the grass shall grow,
Let us know peace.

CHEYENNE NATIVE AMERICAN

Lead me from Death to Life,
from Falsehood to Truth.
Lead me from Despair to Hope,
from Fear to Trust.
Lead me from Hate to Love,
from War to Peace.
Let Peace fill our Heart,
our World, our Universe.

JAINA

With bended knees, with hands outstretched, do I yearn for the effective
expression of the holy spirit working within me:

For this love and understanding, truth and justice; for wisdom to know
the apparent from the real that I might alleviate the sufferings of men
on earth. . . .

God is love, understanding, wisdom, and virtue. Let us love one
another, let us practice mercy and forgiveness, let us have peace, born of
fellow-feeling. . . .

Let my joy be of altruistic living, of doing good to others. Happiness is
unto him from who happiness proceeds to any other human being.

ZOROASTRIAN

O Father, receive Thou the fervor of my soul, the devotion of incarnations, the love of ages that I have kept locked in the vault of my heart.

Divine Father, in my temple of silence I have made a garden for Thee, decorated with the blossoms of my devotion.

With aspiring heart, with zealous mind, with flaming soul, I lay at Thy feet of omnipresence all the flowers of my devotion.

O Spirit, I worship Thee as beauty and intelligence in the temple of nature. I worship Thee as power in the temple of activity, and as peace in the temple of silence.

PARAMAHANSA YOGANANDA

Peace flows through my heart, and blows through me like a zephyr.
Peace fills me like a fragrance.
Peace runs through me like rays.
Peace stabs the heart of noise and worries.
Peace burns through my disquietude.
Peace, like a globe of fire, expands and fills my omnipresence.
Peace, like an ocean, rolls on in all space.
Peace like red blood, vitalizes the veins of my thoughts.
Peace like a boundless aureole, encircles my body of infinity.
Peace-flames blow through the pores of my flesh, and through all space.
The perfume of peace flows over the gardens of blossoms.
The wine of peace runs perpetually through the wine press of all hearts.
Peace is the breath of stones, stars, and sages.
Peace is the ambrosial wine of Spirit flowing from the cask of silence,
Which I quaff with my countless mouths of atoms.

PARAMAHANSA YOGANANDA

My silence, like an expanding sphere, spreads everywhere.

*My silence spreads like a radio song, above, beneath, left and right,
within and without.*

My silence spreads like a wildfire of bliss;

the dark thickets of sorrow and the tall oaks of pride are all burning up.

*My silence, like the ether, passes through everything, carrying the songs
of earth, atoms, and stars into the halls of His infinite mansion.*

PARAMAHANSA YOGANANDA

Sitting still enough I saw nothing coming.
Normal life was hanging like a used shirt,
The sleeves ragged and faded,
The collar ringed.
I expected nothing to visit me that day.
But it arrived like an invisible wind.
From nowhere it touched my forehead.
Whispering in my ear so silently I did not hear.
Tapping my shoulder, less than feather light,
No warning, no presence, nothing more.
It absented me, without I was, like no vacuum,
No hollowness ever evidenced, this was I, gone.
Realizing was wordless and thoughtless, careless.
No investment in keeping, no loss, no gain.
Inside, my chest hovered. Outside, life vibrated,
Buzzing like a famished bee, swarming.
The sting so total, so unlikely, so utterly silent.
There is no imagining this satori, this short samadi.
You cannot go there, meditation brings not it.
It comes, alone and in the night, flannel-footed,
Out of heaven, on the earth, in my heart, God's talk this.

PHILIP DUNN

PRAYERS FOR NATURE

Let my mind bear sweet fruit and fragrant flowers,
as this tree is planted on the soil of Thy spirit.
—with branches downwards:
I see Thy hand
blessing me.
—rising upwards:
Praying for me
with hands raised upwards.
—in the night:
My heart stands in waiting and hope
as the trees stand still through the darkness of night.

HAZRAT INAYAT KHAN

O Lord God of all creation, who stretched forth the heavens and laid
the foundations of the earth, who has appointed the sun to rule by day,
and the moon and stars to rule by night. Thou hast set a boundary to
the sea, and a law for the seasons hast Thou ordained on high; the
wind and the rain obey Thy commands, and the dew of heaven
descends at Thy bidding to moisten the earth. In every time and season
Thou hast made manifest unto us Thy wondrous works; and from festi-
val to festival Thou hast called us to invoke Thy help in the sanctuary,
and to praise Thee in public congregation; for Thou art gracious and
beneficent. We come, therefore, this day to supplicate Thee, and to lay
our petitions before the throne of Thy glory.

JUDAIC PRAYER FOR THE SEASONS

Grandfather, Great Spirit, once more behold me on earth and lean to hear my feeble voice. You lived first, and you are older than all need, older than all prayer. All things belong to you—the two-legged, the four-legged, the wings of the air, and all green things that live.

You have set the powers of the four quarters of the earth to cross each other. You have made me cross the good road, and the road of difficulties, and where they cross, the place is holy. Day in, day out, forevermore, you are the life of things.

BLACK ELK

With the mountains, with the stone
Will I call Thee, Lord, O Lord!
With the birds in the early dawn
Will I call Thee, Lord, O Lord!
With the fishes in the sea,
With gazelles in deserts free,
With the mystic's call "O He!"
Will I call Thee Lord, O Lord!

YUNUS EMRE

PRAYERS FOR TIMES OF THE DAY

O God, you have let me pass the night in peace,
let me pass the day in peace.
Wherever I may go upon my way
which you made peaceable for me,
O God, lead my steps.
When I have spoken, keep lies away from me.
When I am hungry, keep me from murmuring.
When I am satisfied, keep me from pride.
Calling upon you, I pass the day,
O Lord, who has no Lord.

BORAN, PRAYER FOR THE MORNING (KENYA)

O God, you have let me pass this day in peace,
let me pass the night in peace
O Lord who has no Lord,
there is no strength but in thee.
Thou alone hast no obligation.
Under thy hand I pass the night.
Thou art my mother and my father.

BORAN

Lord of Light
help me to know
that you are also
Lord of night
And by your choice
when all is dark
and still and stark
you use your voice.

H. A. WIGGETT

In the morning
God and I meet together
To exchange
Our Compassion and aspiration.
In the evening
God and I meet together
To exchange
Our Forgiveness and gratitude.

SRI CHINMOY

PRAYERS FOR MARRIAGE

May these vows and this marriage be blessed.
May it be sweet milk,
this marriage, like wine and halvah.
May this marriage offer fruit and shade
like the date palm.
May this marriage be full of laughter,
our every day a day of paradise.
May this marriage be a sign of compassion,
a seal of happiness here and hereafter.
May this marriage have a fair face and a good name,
an omen as welcome
as the moon in a clear blue sky.
I am out of words to describe
how spirit mingles in this marriage.

JALAL AL-DIN RUMI

United your resolve,
united your hearts,
may your spirits be at one,
that you may long together dwell
in unity and concord.

THE RIG-VEDA

I honor your gods
I drink at your well
I bring an undefended heart to our meeting place
I have no cherished outcome
I will not negotiate by withholding
I am not subject to disappointment

CELTIC

We swear by peace and love to stand
Heart to heart and hand to hand.
Mark, O Spirit, and hear us now,
Confirming this our Sacred Vow.

DRUID

It is for the union of you and me
that there is light in the sky.
It is for the union of you and me
that the earth is decked in dusky green.
It is for the union of you and me
that the night sits motionless with the world in her arms;
dawn appears opening the eastern door
with sweet murmurs in her voice.
The boat of hope sails along the currents of eternity toward that union,
flowers of the ages are being gathered together for its welcoming ritual.
It is for the union of you and me
that this heart of mine, in the garb of a bride,
has proceeded from birth to birth
upon the surface of this ever-turning world
to choose the beloved.

RABINDRANATH TAGORE

PART THREE

LOCATIONS

FOR PRAYER

❧

Until one is committed, there is hesitancy, the chance to
draw back, always ineffectiveness. Concerning acts of
initiative (and creation) there is one elementary truth the
ignorance of which kills countless ideas and splendid plan:
that the moment one definitely commits oneself then
Providence moves too. All sorts of things occur to help one
that would never have otherwise occurred. A whole stream
of events issues from the decision, raising one's favor all
manner of unforeseen incidents and meetings and material
assistance which no one could have dreamt would come
one's way. Whatever you can do, or dream you can, begin
it. Boldness has genius, power and magic in it.
Begin it now.
JOHANN WOLFGANG VON GOETHE

LOCATIONS FOR PRAYER IN THE UNITED STATES

cx

he following section contains organizations, descriptions, and addresses—divided by denominations—and is intended to provide some of the best and most active prayer locations. It does not offer everything that may be available, but concentrates on a number of very special churches, temples, and centers that are sure to be a bright surprise to anyone who visits.

NON- AND TRANS-DENOMINATIONAL CENTERS

The following are organizations that are interested in the power of prayer, and either do not hold to any particular religious denomination or have a primary passion but allow all others to participate.

SILENT UNITY (NONDENOMINATIONAL)

1901 NW Blue Parkway
Unity Village, MO 64065
Phone: (816) 246-5400
Toll-free: 1-800-669-7729 (within the United States only)
For the hearing-impaired: teletypewriter: (816) 525-1155
Internet address: http://www.unityworldhq.org

This prayer ministry has been conducting prayer on a continuous basis for more than a century—that's prayer nonstop, every day of every week, for more than 100 years! A truly remarkable achievement. It began as a small group of friends and is now a worldwide ministry with hundreds of devoted workers who handle requests for prayer help that arrive in the ministry every day.

Silent Unity conducts a morning prayer meeting every working day to share what they call the Daily Word message. At 11:00 A.M., employees and visitors gather in the chapel for a prayer service. Then there is consecrated prayer at noon and then again at 3:00 and 11:00 P.M. every day.

In addition to these regular gatherings, every half hour throughout the day the workers, one after another, take their turns in the Prayer Vigil Chapel to pray alone. Even at night, the spiritual vigil continues in the small sanctuary. Here in this chapel the prayer requests that are sent in are undertaken beneath the light that beams down from a dome in the roof.

Prayer is held for anyone who requests it, whatever denomination, creed, or location in the world. Each prayer requested is held within the daily vigil for 30 days. There is no counsel given, however, on personal problems, but rather a direction toward God through the constant prayer.

GUIDEPOSTS (CHRISTIAN, TRANS-DENOMINATIONAL)

16 East 34th Street
New York, NY 10016
Phone: 1-800-431-2344

Guideposts is a family of nonprofit organizations that includes **Peale Center**, the **Positive Thinking Foundation**, and **Guideposts Publications**. Together these organizations direct their energies and resources to accomplish a vital mission: to be the world leader in communicating positive, faith-filled principles that empower people to reach their maximum personal and spiritual potential.

Guideposts **magazine**, which was the beginning of the organization, has grown from a 4-page leaflet mailed at irregular intervals to a 48-page, full-color monthly publication reaching more than 16 million people throughout the United States and the world.

The magazine essentially provides readers with true-life stories that offer inspiration for overcoming difficulties and practical suggestions for living a richer and more satisfying life.

The organization is the brainchild of Rev. Norman Vincent Peale, a minister, and Raymond Thornburg, a Pawling, New York, businessman, and was founded in March 1945 as a nondenominational forum for people to relate their inspirational stories intended to provide a "spiritual lift" to all readers.

Another part of the Guideposts organization is the **Peale Center for Christian Living** in Pawling, which offers inspirational publications, audio- and videotapes, seminars, and conferences.

Guideposts Prayer Fellowship uses the power of group prayer to help solve problems and make daily living more effective. Prayer Fellowship responds to more than 8,000 requests monthly.

Dial Guideposts for Inspiration offers two-minute uplifting messages recorded by Rev. Peale and his wife, Ruth Stafford, via daily telephone recordings in 27 cities across the United States. More than 700,000 calls are received annually.

Touchtone for Inspiration features Dr. and Mrs. Peale as well as *Guideposts* authors, who have recorded more than 300 inspirational messages relating to 26 major categories. The service also offers information about outreach programs, and helpful reprints and booklets.

Dial-a-Prayer is a daily message of hope and inspiration followed by a prayer for the day.

At the request of the Salvation Army and other organizations, free publications are provided to those affected in time of national disasters, such as hurricanes and earthquakes.

FIND (Family Information Network Database) is a free confidential service that provides a personalized listing of agencies and programs relating to specific needs.

Guideposts Annual Young Writers Contest offers high school juniors and seniors a total of $20,000 in scholarships for their stories about inspirational personal experiences. How to win a scholarship? Students write honestly and directly about something that has touched them deeply and changed them in some way.

The Writers Workshop, sponsored by *Guideposts* magazine, selects 15 promising writers every two years to attend its weeklong, all-expenses-paid workshop held in Rye, New York.

The School of Practical Christianity brings together clergy and their spouses from the United States and abroad in a nondenominational program of personal growth and spiritual renewal.

THE POSITIVE THINKING FOUNDATION (SECULAR)

Peale Center
66 East Main Street
Pawling, NY 12564
Phone: 1-800-431-2344
Internet address: http://www.guideposts.org

In association with the Peale Center, this secular foundation was established to develop programs and materials for children of all ethnic and religious backgrounds. The foundation produced the "Positive Kids" video program, which has been widely acclaimed and is available in 7,000 public schools around the country.

Designed to help children ages five to nine develop the skills they need to resist negative pressures, the Positive Kids program helps them build self-esteem and develop problem-solving techniques.

AGAPE—SANTA MONICA (CHRISTIAN, TRANS-DENOMINATIONAL)

Agape Church of Religious Science
3211 Olympic Boulevard
Santa Monica, CA 90404
Office address: 1904 Centinela Avenue
Santa Monica, CA 90404
Phone: (310) 829-2780
Tapes of sermons and choir performances: Agape Quiet Mind Bookstore (310) 829-5780
Prayer ministry: (310) 453-6638

Agape International Center of Truth is the home of the Agape Church of Religious Science. It was formed in 1987 as a trans-denominational church with the world as its community.

The church, run by the Reverend Michael Beckwith and his staff, has more than 4,000 active members, 12,000 friends, and 20 ministries and projects dedicated to the realization of the presence of God, peace, and love on this planet, and it is a rapidly growing presence on the West Coast.

Agape is what we might call new age gone mainstream, as it is essentially trans-denominational—that is, although it preaches the teachings of Jesus, it is aware of and interested in all religiousness. It is the largest of 48 Science of Mind churches in greater Los Angeles, which in turn are part of the Religious Science denomination, which includes more than 250 churches worldwide.

Agape is popular with a broad section of the Los Angeles community, including many professionals, actors, musicians, business people, artists, and people looking for something lively. Liveliness they certainly find, as the Sunday service contains gospel music, affirmations, and an inspiring sermon, and the workshops include career enhancement, single parenting, coping with abortion, and many other subjects that will always attract an intelligent and creative crowd, a crowd that is not looking to be judged for their lives.

The Agape Prayer Ministry is a part of the Agape International Center of Truth, with a primary focus on prayer. The practitioners within this aspect of the church engage in prayer as a central feature and are available to answer prayer calls 24 hours a day, seven days a week. The service is free.

CITY OF GOD (TRANS-DENOMINATIONAL)
R.D. 1, Box 319
Moundsville, WV 26041
Phone: N/A

The City of God is a truly unique location and actually constitutes a religious city in West Virginia. Unlike almost all other cities in the world, it is not founded for the purpose of making business but of making love with God. The city is reserved entirely for worshiping and praying with the divine within or between all faiths and traditions, and it is possible to live and work there among the mosques, temples, synagogues, and churches and partake of any of the chants, music, song, and dance.

The founder of the city was Swami Bhaktipada, who was inspired by Srila Prabhupadha, the founder of the Krishna movement in North America, so that the initial roots are Eastern, but the living result is certainly international. The organization became independent from the Hare Krishna movement in 1987 and established religious pluralism and the basic architecture of the City of God as an interfaith concept. There are centers in Florida, New York, and Australia.

GLIDE MEMORIAL CHURCH (TRANS-DENOMINATIONAL, CHRISTIAN METHODIST)

330 Ellis Street
San Francisco, CA 94102
Phone: (415) 771-6300   Fax: (415) 921-6951

Glide Memorial is unique church based on Methodist belief but encourages all other faiths to visit. It operates a strong social and environmental presence in San Francisco, including programs for food, computer tutoring, racial problems, and domestic violence prevention training. The services are fabulous—lively, dramatic, filled with gospel singing and dancing. It's well worth a visit, whatever you believe.

BUDDHIST CENTERS

We have chosen to include some brief résumés of a few locations of special interest that exemplify the Buddhist tradition for prayer in the form of meditation. Following are main Buddhist centers set out according to the different Buddhist denominations, and upon application should provide information regarding prayer or meditation meetings and other gatherings of groups and courses.

THE INSIGHT MEDITATION SOCIETY

1230 Pleasant Street
Barre, MA 01005
Phone: (508) 355-4378   Fax: (508) 355-6398

The Insight Meditation Society is the largest of the American Vipassana centers. It was founded in 1975 to offer retreats to both beginners and experienced meditators, with courses ranging from a weekend to three months, led by one of more than 20 teachers in residence.

A normal day begins with a 5:00 A.M. meditation and ends at 10:00 P.M.; each day is spent in silent practice with sitting and walking meditations. There are also talks and interviews with teachers. Meals are vegetarian and accommodation is very simple.

THE SONOMA MOUNTAIN ZEN CENTER
6367 Sonoma Mount Road
Santa Rosa, CA 95404
Phone: (707) 545-8105

The Sonoma Mountain Zen Center was founded in 1974 and lies in 80 acres of rolling hills and mountainous countryside. The spiritual leader is a Chinese-American named Jakusho Kwong Roshi, and his center offers various retreats with meditation instruction and daily zazen practice.

THE SELF-REALIZATION FELLOWSHIP
3880 San Rafael Avenue
Los Angeles, CA 90065-3298
Phone: (213) 225-2471   Fax: (213) 225-5088

This retreat center was founded in the 1920s by Paramahansa Yogananda, one of the most important and earliest exponents of Raja yoga in the West, and author of *Autobiography of a Yogi*. Raja yoga is a synthesis of other forms of yoga—bhakti and karma yoga, for example—and courses are run within the center for students wishing to discover a lifetime change.

The Self-Realization Fellowship is a worldwide network with more than 400 centers and several retreat centers, including one in Encinitas, California. The headquarters of the Fellowship is in Los Angeles.

Therevada
AMERICAN–SRI LANKA BUDDHIST ASSOCIATION
New York Buddhist Vihara
84-32 124th Street
Kew Gardens, NY 11415
Phone and Fax: (718) 849-2637

VAJIRADHAMMAPADIP TEMPLE
75 California Road
Mt. Vernon, NY 10552-1401
Phone: (914) 699-5778   Fax: (914) 667-1623

BHAVANA SOCIETY
Route 1, Box 218-3
High View, WV 26808
Phone: (304) 856-3241   Fax: (304) 856-2111
E-mail: bhavanasoc@aol.com

Tibetan

THE TIBET CENTER (TIBETAN—GELUG)
359 Broadway, 5th Floor
New York, NY 10013
Phone and Fax: (212) 966-8504

VAJRAPANI INSTITUTE (TIBETAN—GELUG)
Affiliate: Foundation for the Preservation of the Mahayana Tradition
P.O. Box 2130
Boulder Creek, CA 95006
Phone: (408) 338-6654   Fax: (408) 338-3666
E-mail: 76764.2256@compuserve.com

BODHISATTVA INSTITUTE (TIBETAN—KAGYU)
714 North Desert Avenue
Tucson, AZ 85711
Phone: (520) 325-2272   Fax: (520) 326-1678
E-mail: tenpa@azstarnet.com

THE BOULDER SHAMBHALA CENTER/KARMA DZONG
(TIBETAN—KAGYU/NYINGMA)
Affiliate: Shambhala International
1345 Spruce Street
Boulder, CO 80302
Phone: (303) 444-0190   Fax: (303) 443-2975
E-mail: sc@indra.com

RANGRIG YESHE CENTER (TIBETAN—NYINGMA)
P.O. Box 1167
Stockbridge, MA 01262
Phone: (413) 528-9932   Fax: (413) 448-7595

**DZOGCHEN COMMUNITY IN AMERICA-TSEGYALGAR
(TIBETAN—DZOGCHEN)**
Affiliate: International Dzogchen Community
P.O. Box 277
Conway, MA 01341
Phone: (413) 369-4153   Fax: (413) 369-4165
E-mail: 74404.1141@compuserve.com

**VAJRADAKINA BUDDHIST CENTER
(TIBETAN—GELUG)**
Affiliate: New Kadampa Tradition
4915 Junius Street
Dallas, TX 75214
Phone: (214) 823-6385   Fax: (214) 823-6395
E-mail: dakini@waonline.com

**LIGMINCHA INSTITUTE
(TIBETAN—BON)**
P.O. Box 1892
Charlottesville, VA 22903
Phone: (804) 977-6161   Fax: (804) 977-7020
E-mail: ligmincha@aol.com
Internet address: http://www.comet.net/ligmincha

**SAKYA MONASTERY OF TIBETAN BUDDHISM
(TIBETAN—SAKYA AND RIME)**
108 NW 83rd Street
Seattle, WA 98117
Phone: (206) 789-2573   Fax: (206) 789-3994

Vipassana

SPIRIT ROCK MEDITATION CENTER
P.O. Box 909
Woodacre, CA 94973
Phone: (415) 488-0164   Fax: (415) 488-0170
Internet address: http://www.spiritrock.org

INTERNATIONAL MEDITATION CENTER—USA
438 Bankard Road
Westminster, MD 21158
Phone: (410) 346-7889   Fax: (410) 346-7133
E-mail: IMCUSA@compuserve.com

Zen

SAN FRANCISCO ZEN CENTER (ZEN—SOTO)
300 Page Street
San Francisco, CA 94102
Phone: (415) 863-3136   Fax: (415) 431-9220

NEW YORK ZENDO SHOBO-JI (ZEN—RINZAI)
223 East 67th Street
New York, NY 10021
Phone: (212) 861-3333   Fax: (212) 628-6968

ZEN MOUNTAIN MONASTERY (ZEN—SOTO/RINZAI)
P.O. Box 197
South Plank Road
Mt. Tremper, NY 12457
Phone: (914) 688-2228   Fax: (914) 688-2415
E-mail: dharmacom@mhv.net
Internet address: http://www1.mhv.net/dharmacom

ROCHESTER ZEN CENTER
7 Arnold Park
Rochester, NY 14607
Phone: (716) 473-9180   Fax: (716) 473-6846

ZEN BUDDHIST TEMPLE
Affiliate: Buddhist Society for Compassionate Wisdom
1710 West Cornelia Avenue
Chicago, IL 60657-1219
Phone: (312) 528-8685   Fax: (312) 528-9909

FURNACE MOUNTAIN (ZEN—KOREAN)
Affiliate: Kwan Um School
P.O. Box 545
8640 Hardwicks Creek Road
Clay City, KY 40312-0545
Phone: (606) 723-4329

DHARMA RAIN ZEN CENTER (ZEN—SOTO)
2539 SE Madison
Portland, OR 97214
Phone: (503) 239-4846   Fax: (503) 239-5217
E-mail: kyogen@msn.com

**INTERNATIONAL BUDDHIST MEDITATION CENTER
(ZEN—VIETNAMESE)**
928 South New Hampshire Avenue
Los Angeles, CA 90006
Phone: (213) 384-0850   Fax: (213) 386-6643
E-mail: nunk123@ix.netcom.com
Internet address: http://www.cpsc.suu.edu/users/henderso/

MANZANITA VILLAGE (ZEN—VIETNAMESE)
Affiliate: Plum Village, France
P.O. Box 67
Warner Springs, CA 92086
Phone and Fax: (619) 782-9223

ZEN CENTER OF LOS ANGELES (ZEN—SOTO)
923 South Normandie Avenue
Los Angeles, CA 90006-1301
Phone: (213) 387-2351   Fax: (213) 387-2377

SHASTA ABBEY (ZEN—SOTO)
Affiliate: Serene Reflection Meditation Tradition
3612 Summit Drive
P.O. Box 199
Mt. Shasta, CA 96067-0199
Phone: (916) 926-4208   Fax: (916) 926-0428
Internet address: http://www.ONCon.com

Pure Land

NEW YORK BUDDHIST CHURCH (JODO SHINSHU)
331-332 Riverside Drive
New York, NY 10025
Phone: (212) 678-0305   Fax: (212) 662-4502

EKOJI BUDDHIST TEMPLE (JODO SHINSHU)
Affiliate: Buddhist Churches of America
10301 Burke Lake Road
Fairfax Station, VA 22039
Phone: (703) 569-2311
E-mail: tsuji@uno.com

SAGELY CITY OF TEN THOUSAND BUDDHAS (PURE LAND
AND CHAN SCHOOL)
Affiliate: Dharma Realm Buddhist Association
2001 Talmage Road
Talmage, CA 95481-0217
Phone: (707) 462-0939   Fax: (707) 462-0949
E-mail: craig@pacific.net

Nichiren

SOKA GAKKAI INTERNATIONAL-USA (SGI-USA), NICHIREN
National Offices and Center
525 Wilshire Boulevard
Santa Monica, CA 90401
Phone: (310) 260-8900   Fax: (310) 260-8917
E-mail: sgiusa@aol.com
Internet address: http://www.sgi-usa.org

Western Buddhism
SEATTLE BUDDHIST CENTER (FRIENDS OF THE WESTERN BUDDHIST ORDER)
2765 South Washington Street
Seattle, WA 98144
Phone: (206) 726-0051
E-mail: aryadaka@aol.com

CHRISTIAN CENTERS

The following Christian centers, cathedrals, and churches have been chosen both for their special contribution to American prayer and religious gathering and simply as a sampling of the Christian faith in America. There can never be enough locations like these, as they provide for the kind of broad-based and lively religiousness that we have discussed in the first part of this book. Obviously, for anyone searching out locations of Christian prayer, the best place to start is with the local Christian church of whatever denomination appears interesting or attractive. But for those looking for something additional, something dramatic, the following locations are worth even a long journey.

Although we would like to have given the Christian faith complete coverage in this book, it is simply impossible to list so many thousands of different locations and so many variations on the theme of God as expressed through Jesus Christ, so we have chosen a sampling of Episcopal, Lutheran, and Catholic churches. There is additional information about certain locations that are of particular interest, but basic addresses and telephone and fax numbers are given for most.

Episcopal
SAINT JOHN THE DIVINE
1047 Amsterdam Avenue
New York, NY 10025
Phone: (212) 316-7400   Fax: (212) 932-7348

The Dean of Saint John the Divine Cathedral in New York City, James Parks Morton, who, sadly, retired in January 1997, turned one of New York City's most beautiful cathedrals into one of the most innovative places of prayer and worship in the world. Over a period of a quarter century, Dean Morton's Episcopal cathedral became a central point of interfaith celebration and dialogue. Among other things it hosted the interfaith ceremonies for the fiftieth anniversary of the United Nations. Morton also helped found the National Religious Partnership for the Environment and established an artists-in-residence program with artists, writers, and even a high-wire performer named Philippe Petit. He commissioned original works of music, performed each year for the Feast of Saint Francis, which also includes an altar blessing for animals. There is an apprenticeship course for people to learn the ancient art of stone cutting as part of the cathedral's building program.

GRACE CATHEDRAL
1100 California Street
San Francisco, CA 94108
Phone: (415) 749-6300   Fax: (415) 749-6301
Internet address: http://www.gracecom.org.

Grace, as it is known in the San Francisco area, is very similar in its approach to its community as Saint John the Divine in Manhattan. With weekly and even daily events, it undertakes various ministries, including a prison ministry and a health ministry—the two latest. It sponsors artists and holds concerts, special gatherings, and blessings with services for children and animals. There is a food bank for the needy, a support group for gays and lesbians, and the most wonderful festivals at every opportunity. If you're in San Francisco, visiting is a necessity.

ALL SAINTS EPISCOPAL CHURCH
704 South Latah
Boise, ID 83704
Phone: N/A

All Saints Episcopal Church is a member of the Episcopal Community in Boise, Idaho. Whether your background is Protestant or Catholic, you will find commonality in the Episcopal Church. All Saints offers a range of services from the traditional to the modern. The church includes a variety of program music appealing to almost every taste, from traditional choral music to contemporary Christian songs.

CALVARY EPISCOPAL CHURCH
532 Center Street
Santa Cruz, CA 95060
Phone: (408) 423-8787
E-mail: djj@cruzio.com.

THE EPISCOPAL CATHEDRAL CHURCH OF SAINT PAUL
2728 Sixth Avenue
San Diego, CA 92103
Phone: (619) 298-7261   Fax: (619) 298-2689
The Episcopal Cathedral Church of Saint Paul is a unique metropolitan congregation bordering the neighborhoods of Downtown and Hillcrest, situated across the street from historic Balboa Park. The liturgical structure is solidly built on the Anglican tradition of orderly liturgy, strong preaching, and exceptionally sung sacred music. They preach Christ Crucified in an atmosphere of inclusiveness and diversity that clearly defines the nature of the church.

THE EPISCOPAL CHURCH OF SAINT MATTHEW
Baldwin Avenue and El Camino Real
San Mateo, CA 94402
Phone: (415) 342-1481
Originally founded in 1865, the Church of Saint Matthew has a history of service to the San Mateo community for more than 130 years. Saint Matthew's welcomes all visitors and is eager to meet the spiritual needs of all.

THE EPISCOPAL CHURCH OF THE EPIPHANY
2089 Ponce de Leon Avenue NE
Atlanta, GA 30307
Phone: (404) 373-8338

THE EPISCOPAL CHURCH OF THE HEAVENLY REST
602 Meander Street
Abilene, TX 79602
Phone: (915) 677-2091

If you are new to the Episcopal Church, then worship services may seem a little like a juggling contest. This church has a pew sheet to lead you through the service, an insert with the Bible readings, *The Book of Common Prayer*, and the Hymnal for their music.

EPISCOPAL CHURCH OF THE HOLY SPIRIT
12535 Perthshire Road
Houston, TX 77024-4186
Phone: (713) 468-7796
E-mail: ajackson@nettap.com

THE EPISCOPAL CHURCH OF THE TRANSFIGURATION
14115 Hillcrest Road
Dallas, TX 75240-8699
Phone: (972) 233-1898

SAINT ANDREW'S EPISCOPAL CHURCH
1025 Three Mile Road NE
Grand Rapids, MI 49505
Phone: (616) 361-7887

Saint Andrew's is a member of GRACE, the Grand Rapids Area Center for Ecumenism. Nearly 300 congregations participate in some way with the programs of GRACE. Through staff and volunteers, GRACE offers educational resources and programs, opportunities for theological reflection, and activities in the areas of social justice, pastoral care, interfaith issues, and ecumenical worship.

SAINT JAMES' EPISCOPAL CHURCH

222 Eighth Street NE
Washington, DC 20002
Phone: (202) 546-1746

SAINT MARK'S EPISCOPAL CHURCH

10 Saint Mark's Road
Burlington, MA 01803
Phone: (617) 272-1586

The parish of Saint Mark is an Episcopal Church, a member of the Diocese of Massachusetts and the Anglican Communion. Saint Mark's is an inclusive community of more than 200 families and single residents from Burlington and surrounding towns.

SAINT STEPHEN'S EPISCOPAL CHURCH

1935 The Plaza
Schenectady, NY 12309
Phone: (518) 346-6241

This parish is not just a place but a fellowship of Christians attempting to live the faith that they profess. God does not live in buildings, but through people. Saint Stephen's is not where they meet; it is who they are.

SAINT JAMES EPISCOPAL CHURCH

3701 East Martin Luther King Jr. Boulevard
Austin, TX 78721
Phone: (512) 926-6339

SAINT ALBAN'S EPISCOPAL CHURCH

4920 Cline Hollow Road
P.O. Box 466
Murrysville, PA 15668-0466
Phone: (412) 325-2727

Saint Alban's is in the Episcopal Diocese of Pittsburgh. They believe that a congregation should gather in the name of Jesus for praise, prayer, and fellowship. They use Rite II in *The Book of Common Prayer* for Eucharist (The Lord's Supper) services.

Saint Alban's has much more to offer than just Sunday services. They have a strong adult education program and adult bible study. There are weekday and evening programs for children, youth, and adults.

SAINT AMBROSE EPISCOPAL CHURCH

900 Edgewater Boulevard
Foster City, CA 94404
Phone: (415) 574-1369   Fax: (415) 574-5833
E-mail: AmbroseFC@aol.com

SAINT ANDREW'S EPISCOPAL CHURCH

45 Main Street
Newport News, VA 23601
Parish Office: (757) 595-0371
Day School: (757) 595-6261
Fax: (757) 595-0137
E-mail: saec@visi.net

Saint Andrew's church welcomes all people to participate with them in worship, education, and service to the community. Established in 1919, St Andrew's is one of the four original churches formed in Hilton Village. Their mother church is Saint Paul's in downtown Newport News, and they are one of the 124 parishes in the Diocese of southern Virginia under the leadership of Bishop Frank H. Vest.

SAINT JOHN'S IN THE VILLAGE

224 Waverly Place
New York, NY 10014
Phone: (212) 243-6192

Saint John's in the Village has been a witness to the faith in its neighborhood since 1853. At that time most churches had rented pews. But the Free Church of Saint John in the Village was open to all, and that inclusive spirit continues to inspire the church's involvement in the neighborhood and the city.

SAINT LUKE'S ANGLICAN CHURCH
1750 Canby Road
Redding, CA 96002
Phone: (916) 223-0513

Saint Luke's is an Episcopal Church within the Anglican family of churches. They are not, however, affiliated with the Episcopal Church of the United States of America (ECUSA), but are a parish within the Province of Christ the King.

This Province was formed following the Affirmation of Saint Louis in 1977, when traditional Episcopalians became increasingly concerned about fundamental changes to worship, doctrine, and ethics within the ECUSA. They met to reclaim some of the essential timeless beliefs of the church and to form continuing jurisdictions.

In their worship they use the 1928 *Book of Common Prayer*, the King James Bible, and mainly traditional hymns. They enjoy full Apostolic orders through the laying on of hands and the Apostolic Succession.

Saint Luke's has been established in Redding since 1980. It is a small church, but it is growing in numbers and self-confidence. It was founded by Friar Boardman C. Reed (Rector Emeritus), and the current Rector is Fr. Richard Sigrist, who came from the Church of England in 1994.

SAINT MATTHEW AND THE REDEEMER EPISCOPAL CHURCH
825 East Fourth Street
South Boston, MA 02127
Phone: (617) 269-6175

SAINT MICHAEL'S EPISCOPAL CHURCH
110 South Everest Road
P.O. Box 358
Newberg, OR 97132
Phone: (503) 538-3080   Fax: (503) 662-4872

SAINT PETER'S EPISCOPAL CHURCH
4250 North Glebe Road
Arlington, VA 22207
Phone: (703) 536-6606

Lutheran

ABIDING FAITH LUTHERAN CHURCH
3409 Charleston Avenue
Fort Worth, TX 76123
Phone: (817) 294-9303
E-mail: abiding@mail.startext.net

Abiding Faith Lutheran Church is a member of the Wisconsin Evangelical Lutheran Synod, a conservative Lutheran Synod begun in Milwaukee in 1850. Today they are represented in all 50 states and in many other parts of the world.

ALL SAINTS LUTHERAN CHURCH
16510 Mount Oak Road
Bowie, MD 20716
Phone: (301) 249-6300

BETHANY EVANGELICAL LUTHERAN CHURCH
2670 La Tierra Street
Pasadena, CA 91107
Phone: (818) 792-8149

CALVARY LUTHERAN CHURCH
P.O. Box 310
Rio Linda, CA 95673
Phone: (916) 991-2135   E-mail: clc@calweb.com
Internet address: http://www.calweb.com/~clc

CHRIST LUTHERAN CHURCH
222 Niantic Road
Barto, PA 19504
Phone: (610) 845-2583
E-mail: REVPEB@aol.com

FIRST UNITED LUTHERAN CHURCH
6555 Geary Boulevard
San Francisco, CA 94121
Phone: (415) 751-8108   Fax: (415) 751-1080

First United Lutheran Church meets for worship and the celebration of the Eucharist every Sunday morning at 10:00 A.M. They have additional services throughout the church year to celebrate Christmas Eve, Ash Wednesday, Maundy Thursday, Good Friday, and the Vigil of Easter.

While retaining the fundamentally Lutheran elements of the traditional celebration of the mass, the community of First United finds richness, vitality, and spiritual renewal in using a variety of forms and musical settings in their worship celebrations. They therefore have a tradition of changing their musical settings with the various seasons of the church year and frequently use new or different settings within a season or for special celebrations.

Catholic

Atlanta

CORPUS CHRISTI CATHOLIC CHURCH
600 Mountain View Drive
Stone Mountain, GA 30083-3598
Phone: (770) 469-0395

HOLY SPIRIT CATHOLIC CHURCH
4465 Northside Drive NW
Atlanta, GA 30327-3698
Phone: (404) 252-4513

SAINT ANN CATHOLIC CHURCH
4905 Roswell Road
Marietta, GA 30062-6518
Phone: (770) 998-1373

SAINT JOHN THE EVANGELIST CATHOLIC CHURCH
3370 Sunset Street
Hapeville, GA 30354-1653
Phone: (404) 768-5647

SAINT JOSEPH CATHOLIC CHURCH
87 Lacy Street
Marietta, GA 30060-1164
Phone: (770) 422-5633

SAINT JUDE CATHOLIC CHURCH
7171 Glenridge Drive NE
Atlanta, GA 30328-2630
Phone: (770) 394-3896

SAINT THOMAS THE APOSTLE CATHOLIC CHURCH
4300 King Springs Road
Smyrna, GA 30082-4213
Phone: (770) 432-8579

TRANSFIGURATION CATHOLIC CHURCH
1815 Blackwell Road
Marietta, GA 30066-2911
Phone: (770) 977-1442

Baltimore
ALL SAINTS CATHOLIC CHURCH
4408 Liberty Heights Avenue
Baltimore, MD 21207-7593
Phone: (410) 542-0445

ASCENSION CATHOLIC CHURCH
4603 Poplar Avenue
Baltimore, MD 21227-4029
Phone: (410) 242-2292

CATHEDRAL CHURCH OF THE INCARNATION
East University Parkway and Saint Paul Street
Baltimore, MD 21218
Phone: (410) 467-3750

MARY OUR QUEEN CATHEDRAL
5300 North Charles Street
Baltimore, MD 21210-2023
Phone: (410) 433-8800

MOST PRECIOUS BLOOD CATHOLIC CHURCH
5010 Bowleys Lane
Baltimore, MD 21206-6799
Phone: (410) 488-7772

PATRONAGE MOTHER OF GOD BYZANTINE CATHOLIC CHURCH
1260 Stevens Avenue
Baltimore, MD 21227-2644
Phone: (410) 247-4936

SAINT JOHN THE EVANGELIST ROMAN CATHOLIC CHURCH
Wild Lake
Columbia, MD 21044
Phone: (410) 964-1425

SAINT LOUIS CATHOLIC CHURCH
12500 Clarksville Pike
Columbia, MD 21044
Phone: (410) 531-6040

SAINT MICHAEL'S UKRAINIAN CATHOLIC CHURCH
2401 Eastern Avenue
Baltimore, MD 21224-3613
Phone: (410) 675-7557

SAINT PETER AND PAUL'S UKRAINIAN CATHOLIC CHURCH
1506 Church Street
Baltimore, MD 21226-1489
Phone: (410) 355-3578

SAINT PETER CLAVER CATHOLIC CHURCH
1546 North Fremont Avenue
Baltimore, MD 21217-2817
Phone: (410) 728-2023

Chicago

APOSTOLIC CATHOLIC ASSYRIAN CHURCH
7201 North Ashland Boulevard
Chicago, IL 60626-2503
Phone: (312) 465-4777

CATHOLIC CATHEDRAL OF THE HOLY NAME
735 North State Street
Chicago, IL 60610-3835
Phone: (312) 787-8040

KOREAN CATHOLIC CHURCH
4115 North Kedvale Avenue
Chicago, IL 60641-2247
Phone: (312) 283-3979

LIBERAL CATHOLIC CHURCH OF SAINT FRANCIS
1945 North Mozart Street
Chicago, IL 60647-3932
Phone: (312) 489-0440

SACRED HEART CATHOLIC CHURCH
905 Burr Avenue
Winnetka, IL 60093-1750
Phone: (708) 446-0856

SAINT FRANCIS XAVIER CATHOLIC CHURCH
524 9th Street
Wilmette, IL 60091-2714
Phone: (708) 256-4250

SAINT GEORGE ROMAN CATHOLIC CHURCH
9546 South Ewing Avenue
Chicago, IL 60617-5195
Phone: (312) 734-9468

SAINT JAMES CATHOLIC CHURCH
2942 South Wabash Avenue
Chicago, IL 60616-3293
Phone: (312) 842-1919

SAINT JAMES CATHOLIC CHURCH
820 North Arlington Heights Road
Arlington Heights, IL 60004-5699
Phone: (708) 253-6305

SAINT JULIAN EYMARD CATHOLIC CHURCH
601 Biesterfield Road
Elk Grove Village, IL 60007-3308
Phone: (708) 956-0130

SAINT LUKE ROMAN CATHOLIC CHURCH
520 Lathrop Avenue
Oak Park, IL 60301
Phone: (708) 771-8250

SAINT MARY'S BYZANTINE CATHOLIC CHURCH
4949 South Seeley Avenue
Chicago, IL 60609-4713
Phone: (312) 434-1710

SAINT MATTHEW CATHOLIC CHURCH
1001 East Schaumburg Road
Schaumburg, IL 60172
Phone: (708) 893-1220

SAINT MICHAEL CATHOLIC CHURCH
315 West Illinois Street
Wheaton, IL 60187-5090
Phone: (708) 665-2250

SAINT MICHAEL UKRAINIAN CATHOLIC CHURCH
12211 South Parnell Avenue
Chicago, IL 60628-6405
Phone: (312) 785-7443

SAINT PETER'S CATHOLIC CHURCH
8116 Niles Center Road
Lincolnwood, IL 60645
Phone: (708) 673-1492

SAINT PETRONILLE CATHOLIC CHURCH
420 Glenwood Avenue
Glen Ellyn, IL 60137-4588
Phone: (708) 469-0404

SAINT PHILIP THE APOSTLE ROMAN CATHOLIC CHURCH
1223 West Holtz Avenue
Addison, IL 60101-2199
Phone: (708) 628-0900

SAINT STEPHEN CATHOLIC CHURCH
1267 Everett Avenue
Des Plaines, IL 60018-2398
Phone: (708) 824-2026

SAINT THERESA CATHOLIC CHURCH
467 North Benton Street
Palatine, IL 60067-3583
Phone: (708) 358-7760

Dallas–Fort Worth
ALL SAINTS CATHOLIC CHURCH
5231 Meadowcreek Drive
Dallas, TX 75248-4095
Phone: (214) 661-0490

ALL SAINTS CATHOLIC CHURCH
214 Northwest 20th Street
Fort Worth, TX 76106-8199
Phone: (817) 626-3055

HOLY CROSS CATHOLIC CHURCH
4910 Bonnie View Road
Dallas, TX 75241-1601
Phone: (214) 375-7457

MOST BLESSED SACRAMENT CATHOLIC CHURCH IN ARLINGTON
2100 North Davis Drive
Arlington, TX 76012-1803
Phone: (817) 460-2751

OUR LADY QUEEN OF PEACE
807 Thomasson Drive
Dallas, TX 75208-3955
Phone: (214) 942-2129

SAINT ANDREW KIM CATHOLIC CHURCH
2712 Swiss Avenue
Dallas, TX 75204-5996
Phone: (214) 651-9150

SAINT MARIA GORETTI CATHOLIC CHURCH
1200 South Davis Drive
Arlington, TX 76013-2399
Phone: (817) 274-0643

SAINT PATRICK'S CATHEDRAL
1206 Throckmorton Street
Fort Worth, TX 76102-6308
Phone: (817) 332-4915

SAINT PETER THE APOSTLE CATHOLIC CHURCH
1201 South Cherry Lane
Fort Worth, TX 76108-3297
Phone: (817) 246-0011

SAINT PIUS X CHURCH
3030 Gus Thomasson Road
Dallas, TX 75228-3104
Phone: (214) 279-6155

SAINT RITA'S CATHOLIC CHURCH
5550 East Lancaster Avenue
Fort Worth, TX 76112-6429
Phone: (817) 451-9395

SAINT THOMAS CHURCH
2920 Azle Avenue
Fort Worth, TX 76106-4909
Phone: (817) 624-2184

SAINT VINCENT DE PAUL CATHOLIC CHURCH
5819 West Pleasant Ridge Road
Arlington, TX 76016-4499
Phone: (817) 478-8206

SAN MATEO CATHOLIC CHURCH
2909 Photo Avenue
Fort Worth, TX 76107-5707
Phone: (817) 737-5470

Miami

ANNUNCIATION CATHOLIC CHURCH
3781 Southwest 39th Street
Hollywood, FL 33023-6252
Phone: (954) 989-0606

ASSUMPTION CATHOLIC CHURCH
2001 South Ocean Boulevard
Pompano Beach, FL 33062-8099
Phone: (954) 941-7647

BLESSED SACRAMENT CATHOLIC CHURCH
1701 East Oakland Park Boulevard
Oakland Park, FL 33334-5238
Phone: (954) 564-1010

HOLY FAMILY CATHOLIC CHURCH
14500 Northeast 11th Avenue
Miami, FL 33161-2499
Phone: (305) 947-1471

HOLY REDEEMER ROMAN CATHOLIC CHURCH
1301 Northwest 71st Street
Miami, FL 33147-7000
Phone: (305) 691-1701

HOLY ROSARY CATHOLIC CHURCH
9500 Southwest 184th Street
Miami, FL 33157-7019
Phone: (305) 235-5135

IMMACULATE CONCEPTION CATHOLIC CHURCH
4497 West 1st Avenue
Hialeah, FL 33012-4016
Phone: (305) 822-2011

KOREAN CATHOLIC CHURCH
3600 Southwest 32nd Boulevard
Hollywood, FL 33023-6316
Phone: (954) 986-9960

MOTHER OF OUR REDEEMER CATHOLIC CHURCH
18295 Northwest 68th Avenue
Hialeah, FL 33015-3404
Phone: (305) 558-4404

SAINT AGATHA CATHOLIC CHURCH
1111 Southwest 107th Avenue
Miami, FL 33174-2599
Phone: (305) 222-1500

SAINT ANDREW'S CATHOLIC CHURCH
9950 Northwest 29th Avenue
Miami, FL 33147-2010
Phone: (954) 752-3950

SAINT BENEDICT CATHOLIC CHURCH
7750 West 7th Avenue
Hialeah, FL 33014-4118
Phone: (305) 558-2150

SAINT BERNADETTE CATHOLIC CHURCH
7450 Stirling Road
Hollywood, FL 33024-1513
Phone: (954) 432-5313

SAINT BONIFACE CATHOLIC CHURCH
8330 Johnson Street
Pembroke Pines, FL 33024-6699
Phone: (954) 432-2750

SAINT BRENDAN CATHOLIC CHURCH
8725 Southwest 32nd Street
Miami, FL 33165-3292
Phone: (305) 221-0881

SAINT CECILIA CATHOLIC CHURCH
1040 West 29th Street
Hialeah, FL 33010
Phone: (305) 885-4614

SAINT CHARLES BORROMEO CATHOLIC CHURCH
123 Northwest 6th Avenue
Hallandale, FL 33009-4127
Phone: (954) 458-1914

SAINT ELIZABETH CATHOLIC CHURCH
3331 Northeast 10th Terrace
Pompano Beach, FL 33064-5298
Phone: (954) 943-6801

SAINT FRANCIS DE SALES CATHOLIC CHURCH
600 Lenox Avenue
Miami Beach, FL 33139-5907
Phone: (305) 672-0093

SAINT GABRIEL CATHOLIC CHURCH
731 North Ocean Boulevard
Pompano Beach, FL 33062-4634
Phone: (954) 943-3684

SAINT GEORGE CATHOLIC CHURCH
3640 Northwest 8th Street
Fort Lauderdale, FL 33311-6418
Phone: (305) 583-5892

SAINT GREGORY CATHOLIC CHURCH
200 North University Drive
Plantation, FL 33324-2018
Phone: (954) 473-6261

SAINT HELEN'S ROMAN CATHOLIC CHURCH
3033 Northwest 33rd Avenue
Fort Lauderdale, FL 33311-1123
Phone: (954) 731-7314

SAINT JOHN THE APOSTLE CATHOLIC CHURCH
475 East 4th Street
Hialeah, FL 33010-5009
Phone: (305) 888-9769

SAINT JOHN THE BAPTIST CATHOLIC CHURCH
4595 Bayview Drive
Fort Lauderdale, FL 33308-5330
Phone: (954) 771-8950

SAINT JOSEPH'S CATHOLIC CHURCH
8670 Byron Avenue
Miami Beach, FL 33141-4805
Phone: (305) 866-6567

SAINT JUDE MELKITE CATHOLIC CHURCH
126 Southeast 15th Road
Miami, FL 33010
Phone: (305) 856-1500

SAINT KEVIN ROMAN CATHOLIC CHURCH
12525 Southwest 42nd Street
Miami, FL 33175-2999
Phone: (305) 223-0633

SAINT KIERAN'S CATHOLIC CHURCH
3605 South Miami Avenue
Miami, FL 33133-4205
Phone: (305) 854-1521

SAINT LAWRENCE CATHOLIC CHURCH
2200 Northeast 191st Street
Miami, FL 33180-2199
Phone: (305) 932-3560

SAINT LOUIS CATHOLIC CHURCH
7270 Southwest 120th Street
Miami, FL 33156-4659
Phone: (305) 238-7562

SAINT MALACHY CATHOLIC CHURCH
6200 John Horan Terrace
Tamarac, FL 33321-6000
Phone: (954) 726-1237

SAINT MARK CATHOLIC CHURCH
5601 South Flamingo Road
Fort Lauderdale, FL 33330-3203
Phone: (954) 434-3777

SAINT MAURICE CATHOLIC CHURCH
2851 Stirling Road
Hollywood, FL 33020
Phone: (954) 961-7777

SAINT MAXIMILIAN KOLBE CATHOLIC CHURCH
11051 Northwest 16th Street
Hollywood, FL 33026-2721
Phone: (954) 432-0206

SAINT MICHAEL'S CATHOLIC CHURCH
2987 West Flagler Street
Miami, FL 33010
Phone: (305) 649-1811

SAINT PETER AND PAUL CATHOLIC CHURCH
900 Southwest 26th Road
Miami, FL 33129-2299
Phone: (305) 858-2621

SAINT PETER'S AFRICAN ORTHODOX CATHOLIC CHURCH
4841 Northwest 2nd Avenue
Miami, FL 33127-2429
Phone: (305) 759-0314

SAINT PETER'S ORTHODOX CATHOLIC CHURCH
1811 Northwest 4th Court
Miami, FL 33136-1201
Phone: (305) 573-8941

SAINT PHILOMENA CATHOLIC CHURCH
1621 Southwest 6th Street
Miami, FL 33010
Phone: (305) 644-1400

SAINT SEBASTIAN CATHOLIC CHURCH
2000 Southeast 25th Avenue
Fort Lauderdale, FL 33316-3226
Phone: (954) 524-9344

SAINT STEPHEN CATHOLIC CHURCH
6044 Southwest 19th Street
Miramar, FL 33023-2913
Phone: (954) 987-1100

SAINT THOMAS THE APOSTLE CATHOLIC CHURCH
7303 Southwest 64th Street
Miami, FL 33143-2946
Phone: (305) 665-5600

SANTA BARBARA CATHOLIC CHURCH
11960 Northwest 87th Court
Hialeah, FL 33016-1977
Phone: (305) 558-7256

VISITATION CATHOLIC CHURCH
100 Northeast 191st Street
Miami, FL 33179-3711
Phone: (305) 652-3624

Phoenix
ALL SAINTS CATHOLIC CHURCH
1534 North Recker Road
Mesa, AZ 85205-4410
Phone: (602) 985-7655

ALL SAINTS NEWMAN CATHOLIC CENTER
230 East University Drive
Tempe, AZ 85281-3730
Phone: (602) 967-7823

BLESSED SACRAMENT CATHOLIC CHURCH
11300 North 64th Street
Scottsdale, AZ 85254-5007
Phone: (602) 948-8370

CHRIST THE KING CATHOLIC CHURCH
1505 East Dana Avenue
Mesa, AZ 85204-1214
Phone: (602) 964-1719

CORPUS CHRISTI CATHOLIC CHURCH
3550 East Knox Road
Phoenix, AZ 85044-3500
Phone: (602) 893-8770

HOLY CROSS CATHOLIC CHURCH
1244 South Power Road
Mesa, AZ 85206-3702
Phone: (602) 981-2021

HOLY FAMILY CATHOLIC CHURCH
6802 South 24th Street
Phoenix, AZ 85040-5804
Phone: (602) 268-2632

SAINT ANDREW THE APOSTLE CATHOLIC CHURCH
3450 West Ray Road
Chandler, AZ 85226-2300
Phone: (602) 899-1990

SAINT ANNE'S CATHOLIC CHURCH
440 East Elliot Road
Mesa, AZ 85204
Phone: (602) 892-4970

SAINT ANTHONY CATHOLIC CHURCH
909 South 1st Avenue
Phoenix, AZ 85003-2505
Phone: (602) 252-1771

SAINT BRIDGET CATHOLIC CHURCH
2213 North Lindsay Road
Mesa, AZ 85213-2317
Phone: (602) 924-9111

SAINT CLEMENT'S CATHOLIC CHURCH
15800 North Del Webb Boulevard
Sun City, AZ 85351-1698
Phone: (602) 974-5867

SAINT DANIEL'S CATHOLIC CHURCH
7923 East Latham Street
Scottsdale, AZ 85257-3737
Phone: (602) 945-8437

SAINT EDWARD'S CATHOLIC CHURCH
4410 East Southern Avenue
Tempe, AZ 85282
Phone: (602) 438-0043

SAINT JAMES CATHOLIC CHURCH
19640 North 35th Avenue
Glendale, AZ 85308-2202
Phone: (602) 581-0707

SAINT LUKE'S CATHOLIC CHURCH
19644 North 7th Avenue
Phoenix, AZ 85027-4748
Phone: (602) 582-0561

SAINT MARK'S CATHOLIC CHURCH
400 North 30th Street
Phoenix, AZ 85008-6198
Phone: (602) 267-0503

SAINT MARY'S BASILICA CATHOLIC CHURCH
231 North 3rd Street
Phoenix, AZ 85004-2219
Phone: (602) 252-7651

SAINT RAPHAEL'S CATHOLIC CHURCH
5524 West Acoma Drive
Glendale, AZ 85306-4202
Phone: (602) 938-4227

SAINT WILLIAM'S CATHOLIC CHURCH
11025 West 3 Street
Cashion, AZ 85329
Phone: (602) 936-6115

SANTA TERESITA CATHOLIC CHURCH
14016 North Verbena Street
El Mirage, AZ 85335
Phone: (602) 583-8183

UKRAINIAN CATHOLIC CHURCH
3720 West Maryland Avenue
Glendale, AZ 85301
Phone: (602) 973-0810

San Diego
ALL HALLOWS CATHOLIC CHURCH
6590 La Jolla Scenic Drive South
La Jolla, CA 92092
Phone: (619) 459-2975

ASCENSION CATHOLIC PARISH
11292 Clairemont Mesa Boulevard
San Diego, CA 92124-1524
Phone: (619) 279-2735

BLESSED SACRAMENT CATHOLIC CHURCH
4540 El Cerrito Drive
San Diego, CA 92115-3797
Phone: (619) 582-5722

HOLY FAMILY CATHOLIC CHURCH
1957 Coolidge Street
San Diego, CA 92111-7098
Phone: (619) 277-0404

HOLY SPIRIT CATHOLIC CHURCH
2725 55th Street
San Diego, CA 92105-5095
Phone: (619) 262-2435

IMMACULATA CATHOLIC CHURCH
Linda Vista Road and Alcala Park
San Diego, CA 92103
Phone: (619) 293-3358

IMMACULATE CONCEPTION CHURCH, OLD TOWN
2540 San Diego Avenue
San Diego, CA 92110-2840
Phone: (619) 295-4148

OUR LADY OF GRACE CATHOLIC CHURCH
2766 Navajo Road
El Cajon, CA 92020-2183
Phone: (619) 469-0133

OUR LADY OF GUADALUPE CATHOLIC CHURCH
345 Anita Street
Chula Vista, CA 91911-4198
Phone: (619) 422-3977

OUR LADY OF GUADALUPE CATHOLIC CHURCH
1770 Kearney Avenue
San Diego, CA 92113-1128
Phone: (619) 233-3838

OUR LADY OF MOUNT CARMEL CHURCH
13541 Stony Creek Road
San Diego, CA 92129-2099
Phone: (619) 566-3550

OUR LADY OF REFUGE CHURCH
4212 Jewell
La Jolla, CA 92093
Phone: (619) 273-9377

OUR LADY OF THE ROSARY CATHOLIC CHURCH
1659 Columbia Street
San Diego, CA 92101-2501
Phone: (619) 234-4820

OUR LADY OF THE SACRED HEART CATHOLIC CHURCH
4177 Marlborough Avenue
San Diego, CA 92105-1412
Phone: (619) 280-0515

SACRED HEART CHURCH
4776 Saratoga Avenue
San Diego, CA 92107-2296
Phone: (619) 224-2746

SAINT AGNES CATHOLIC CHURCH
1140 Evergreen Street
San Diego, CA 92106-2532
Phone: (619) 223-2200

SAINT ANNE'S CATHOLIC CHURCH
621 Sicard Street
San Diego, CA 92113-2334
Phone: (619) 239-8253

SAINT ANTHONY'S CATHOLIC CHURCH
1816 Harding Avenue
National City, CA 91950-5534
Phone: (619) 477-4520

SAINT BRIGID CATHOLIC CHURCH
4735 Cass Street
San Diego, CA 92109-2602
Phone: (619) 483-3030

SAINT CATHERINE LABOURE CATHOLIC CHURCH
Mount Alifan Drive and Mount Abraham Avenue
San Diego, CA 92123
Phone: (619) 277-3133

SAINT DIDACUS CATHOLIC CHURCH
4772 Felton Street
San Diego, CA 92116-1824
Phone: (619) 284-3472

SAINT FRANCIS LIBERAL CATHOLIC CHURCH
741 Cerro Gordo Avenue
San Diego, CA 92102-2711
Phone: (619) 239-0637

SAINT GABRIEL CATHOLIC CHURCH OF POWAY
13734 Twin Peaks Road
Poway, CA 92064-3036
Phone: (619) 748-5348

SAINT JAMES CATHOLIC CHURCH
625 South Nardo Avenue
Solana Beach, CA 92075-2398
Phone: (619) 755-2545

SAINT JOHN'S CATHOLIC CHURCH
1001 Encinitas Boulevard
Encinitas, CA 92024-2828
Phone: (619) 753-6254

SAINT JOHN'S CATHOLIC CHURCH
1638 Polk Avenue
San Diego, CA 92103-2622
Phone: (619) 291-1660

SAINT LEO MISSION CHURCH
936 Genevieve Street
Solana Beach, CA 92075-2070
Phone: (619) 481-6788

SAINT LOUISE DE MARILLAC CATHOLIC CHURCH
2005 Crest Drive
El Cajon, CA 92021-4309
Phone: (619) 444-3076

SAINT MARTIN'S CATHOLIC CHURCH
7710 El Cajon Boulevard
La Mesa, CA 91941-4932
Phone: (619) 465-5334

SAINT MICHAEL'S CATHOLIC CHURCH
2643 Homedale
National City, CA 91950
Phone: (619) 470-1977

SAINT MICHAEL'S CATHOLIC CHURCH OF POWAY
15546 Pomerado Road
Poway, CA 92064-2404
Phone: (619) 487-4755

Washington, D.C.
ASCENSION CATHOLIC CHURCH
12700 Lanham Severn Road
Bowie, MD 20720-4566
Phone: (301) 262-2227

BLESSED SACRAMENT CATHOLIC CHURCH
1417 West Braddock Road
Alexandria, VA 22302-2707
Phone: (703) 998-6100

CATHEDRAL OF SAINT THOMAS MORE
3838 North Cathedral Lane
Arlington, VA 22201
Phone: (703) 525-1300

EPIPHANY BYZANTINE CATHOLIC CHURCH
3410 Woodburn Road
Annandale, VA 22003-1370
Phone: (703) 573-3986

GOOD SHEPHERD CATHOLIC CHURCH
8710 Mount Vernon Highway
Alexandria, VA 22309-2238
Phone: (703) 780-4055

HOLY FAMILY CATHOLIC CHURCH
12010 Woodmore Road
Bowie, MD 20721-4106
Phone: (301) 249-1167

SAINT AGNES CATHOLIC CHURCH
1914 North Randolph Street
Arlington, VA 22207-3046
Phone: (703) 525-1166

SAINT CATHERINE OF SIENA CATHOLIC CHURCH
1020 Springvale Road
Great Falls, VA 22066-1738
Phone: (703) 759-4350

SAINT CHARLES CATHOLIC CHURCH
3304 North Washington Boulevard
Arlington, VA 22201-4599
Phone: (703) 527-5500

SAINT EDWARD'S CATHOLIC CHURCH
1940 Mitchvale Road
Bowie, MD 20715
Phone: (301) 249-9599

SAINT JAMES CATHOLIC CHURCH
905 Park Avenue
Falls Church, VA 22046-3104
Phone: (703) 532-8815

SAINT JAMES CATHOLIC CHURCH
3628 Ri Avenue
Hyattsville, MD 20780
Phone: (301) 927-0567

SAINT JOHN NEUMANN CATHOLIC CHURCH
9000 Warfield Road
Gaithersburg, MD 20877
Phone: (301) 840-9682

SAINT LEO'S CATHOLIC CHURCH
3700 Old Lee Highway
Fairfax, VA 22030-1889
Phone: (703) 273-5369

SAINT LOUIS CATHOLIC CHURCH
2907 Popkins Lane
Alexandria, VA 22306-1887
Phone: (703) 765-4421

SAINT LUKE'S CATHOLIC CHURCH
7001 Georgetown Pike
McLean, VA 22101-2150
Phone: (703) 356-1255

SAINT MARK'S CATHOLIC CHURCH
9970 Vale Road
Vienna, VA 22181-4005
Phone: (703) 938-3293

SAINT MARY'S CATHOLIC CHURCH
5222 Sideburn Road
Fairfax, VA 22032-2640
Phone: (703) 978-4141

SAINT PATRICK'S CATHOLIC CHURCH
619 10th Street Northwest
Washington, DC 20001-4509
Phone: (202) 347-2713

SAINT PHILIP'S CATHOLIC CHURCH
Camp Alger Avenue and Saint Philip's Court
Falls Church, VA 22046
Phone: (703) 573-3808

SAINT THOMAS MORE CATHEDRAL
3901 Cathedral Lane
Arlington, VA 22203-3600
Phone: (703) 525-1300

Christian Meditation Centers

Christian meditation centers can be found throughout the world and practice a Christian meditation originally created by John Main. The following centers operate retreats, details of which can be found on application.

THE CHRISTIAN MEDITATION CENTER
4b 322 East 49th Street
New York, NY 10017
Phone: (212) 831-5710

THE CHRISTIAN MEDITATION CENTER
1130 Westchester Place
Los Angeles, CA 90019
Phone: (209) 897-3711

OSAGE MONASTERY
1870 West Monastery Road
Sand Springs, OK 74063
Phone: (918) 245-2734

OUR LADY OF GUADALOUPE TRAPPIST ABBEY (INTERFAITH)
P.O. Box 97
Lafayette, OR 97127
Phone: (503) 852-0107

JEWISH SYNAGOGUES

There are hundreds of wonderful and welcoming Jewish centers in America. The following were chosen because I have visited them at one time or another and felt them to be particularly beautiful, either in their locations or in some aspect of the work that they are doing.

ADAT ARI EL

12020 Burbank Boulevard (at Laurel Canyon)
North Hollywood, CA 91607
Phone: (213) 877-0666

Adat Ari El means "Congregation of the Lion of God." It is a conservative congregation, committed to traditional Jewish law and practice.

For more than 50 years, Adat Ari El has enhanced the awareness and appreciation of Jewish ethical values and rituals through the celebration and observance of life cycle events. Like the holy city of Jerusalem, Adat Ari El has many gates through which people can enter its community. Some find their way through the Shabbat service, some through the schools, some through the daily minyan, some through youth programs, some through the special programs, such as the Ashkenazic Faire, Havdalah at the Los Angeles Zoo, or musical concerts.

CONGREGATION BETH SHOLOM

1301 Clement Street (at 14th Avenue)
P.O. Box 590418
San Francisco, CA 94159-0418
Phone: (415) 221-8736

Congregation Beth Sholom is a traditional conservative egalitarian congregation affiliated with the United Synagogue of Conservative Judaism and its Northern California Region.

CONGREGATION BONAI SHALOM

1527 Cherryvale Road
Boulder, CO 80303
Phone: (303) 442-6605

Congregation Bonai Shalom, founded in 1981, is an egalitarian Conservative synagogue affiliated with the United Synagogue of Conservative Judaism.

CONGREGATION RODFEI ZEDEK

5200 South Hyde Park Boulevard
Chicago, IL 60615
Phone: (773) 752-2770   Fax: (773) 752-0330

ADATH JESHURUN
2401 Woodbourne Avenue
Louisville, KY 40205
Phone: (502) 458-5359   Fax: (502) 451-5634
Internet address: http://uscj.org/ohio/louisvca

BETH SHALOM
9400 Wornall Road
Kansas City, MO 64114
Phone: (816) 361-2990   Fax: (816) 361-4495
E-mail: bethshal@sound.net

Since 1878, Beth Shalom has been a Conservative congregation with a rich heritage in Kansas City. Currently, the congregation of 1,200 families holds services and programs encompassing the wide spectrum of Jewish religious, cultural, educational, and social experiences. Specialty programs occur for different age groups and for special events.

TEMPLE BETH-EL
338 Walnut Avenue
Cranford, NJ 07016
Phone: (908) 276-9231   Fax: (908) 276-6570

BELLMORE JEWISH CENTER
2550 South Centre Avenue
Bellmore, NY 11710
Phone: (516) 781-3072

HILLCREST JEWISH CENTER
183-02 Union Turnpike
Flushing, NY 11366
Phone: (718) 380-4145

Hillcrest Jewish Center, affiliated with the United Synagogue of Conservative Judaism, was founded in 1939.

ANSCHE CHESED
251 West 100th Street
New York, NY 10025
Phone: (212) 865-0600
E-mail: bogursky@panix.com

THE CONSERVATIVE SYNAGOGUE OF FIFTH AVENUE
11 East 11th Street
New York, NY 10003
Phone: (212) 929-6954   Fax: (212) 929-0151

TEMPLE BETH-EL
139 South Winton Road
Rochester, NY 14610-2997
Phone: (716) 473-1770   Fax: (716) 473-2689

Since its founding in 1915, Temple Beth-El has been guided by dedicated and highly motivated professional and laypeople constantly seeking better ways of meeting the needs of its congregants. Temple Beth-El invites and welcomes visitors and guests to join them in their daily and Sabbath services.

GERMANTOWN JEWISH CENTRE
400 West Ellet Street
Philadelphia, PA 19119
Phone: (215) 844-1507   Fax: (215) 844-8309

This Jewish congregation, affiliated with the United Synagogue of Conservative Judaism, has been at the heart of the Jewish community in northwest Philadelphia and the surrounding suburbs for more than 60 years. A vital presence in the region, Germantown Jewish Centre has consistently served the spiritual, educational, social, and cultural needs of the Jews and their families. At the same time, it has preserved and enriched the community for people of all faiths.

A congregation where women and men participate as equals, Germantown Jewish Centre is affiliated with the Conservative Movement and takes a progressive approach to ritual observance and synagogue life.

CONGREGATION AGUDAS ACHIM
4300 Bull Creek Road
Austin, TX 78756-5999
Phone: (512) 459-3287

Congregation Agudas Achim is affiliated with the Conservative Movement. They offer a wide range of religious, educational, community service, cultural, and social activities.

BETH-EL NER TAMID SYNAGOGUE
2900 West Mequon Road
Mequon, WI 53092
Phone: (414) 242-6900   Fax: (414) 242-3952

HINDU CENTERS

There are many Hindu temples and centers in the United States. Although Hinduism has not yet gained the popularity with Western seekers in America that Buddhism has, it is of the greatest fascination to anyone searching for beauty, originality, and spiritual fulfillment. Born from the most ancient of religions, Vedism, Hinduism contains hundreds of variations and thousands of gods and goddesses, and can be deeply confusing at the outset. The best approach is not to try to "understand" in the Western, rational fashion, but simply to watch, taste, and smell the incredible beauty of this vastly varied love affair with the divine, within which the central aspect is prayer. Here are some centers of interest.

THE SOCIETY OF ABIDANCE IN TRUTH (SAT)
1834 Ocean Street
Santa Cruz, CA 95060
Phone: (408) 425-7287
E-mail: RAMANA@cruzio.com

The Society of Abidance in Truth (SAT) is consecrated to Advaita Vedanta as revealed by Bhagavan Sri Ramana Maharishi. There are meditation retreats and book lists, and satsang (sitting at the feet of the master) is held on a regular basis.

HINDU TEMPLE SOUTH-BAY
450 Persian Drive
Sunnyvale, CA 94089
Phone: (408) 734-4554
For Bookings: (408) 741-1162 or (408) 238-8975

HINDU COMMUNITY AND CULTURAL CENTER
1232 Arrowhead Avenue
Livermore, CA 94550
Phone: (510) 449-6255   Fax: (510) 455-0404

CHINMAYA MISSION
Sandeepany, 1050 Park Avenue
San Jose, CA 95126
Phone: (408) 998-2793

THE HINDU TEMPLE SOCIETY OF NORTH AMERICA
SRI MAHA VALLABHA GANAPATI DEVASTHANAM
45-57 Bowne Street
Flushing, NY 11355
Phone: (718) 460-8484
Toll-free: 1-800-99HINDU
Fax: (718) 461-8055
E-mail: ganesh@indianet.com.

The logo of the Society, adapted from Sri Satya Sai Baba's ecumenical symbol, is a light surrounded by insignias of several religions with the OM symbol on top. It signifies the universality, catholicity, and spirit of tolerance of Hinduism. While stressing the supremacy of the Absolute and deifying some of the major aspects as represented by the main deities, the Center stresses the totality and fundamental unity at the core of all religion. The Temple provides a spectrum of approaches to God.

SRI VENKATESWARA SWAMI TEMPLE OF GREATER CHICAGO
1145 West Sullivan Road
Aurora, IL 60507
Phone: (708) 844-2252   Fax: (708) 844-2254
E-mail: balaji@balaji.org

NATIVE AMERICAN, SHAMANIC, AND WICCAN CENTERS

Native American, Shaman, and Wicca religions have increased in popularity since the 1960s, partly due to exponents such as Carlos Castaneda and the Mexican teacher Don Juan, but also because of our need to return to our religious roots and our increasing disillusionment with traditional religions. Shamanism is as old as the Vedas, and older than Judaism, and there are many centers in the United States that cater to the inquisitive spirit that wishes to sample the sweat lodge and the Kahuna. Following are a few samples.

CIRCLE SANCTUARY

P.O. Box 219
Mt. Horeb, WI 53572
Phone: (608) 924-2216   Fax: (608) 924-5961

This is an international center for nature spirituality and a Shamanic Wicca church. Its main center is situated on a sacred nature preserve near Mt. Horeb in the forests of southwest Wisconsin. Its facilities include research, counseling, healing, education, nature preservation, and interfaith dialogue. It also operates Circle Network, which aims to link thousands of people, groups, centers, and other networks with a variety of periodicals, directories, and news journals. There are seasonal gatherings, festivals, rituals, moon circles, meditations, and workshops held at the Circle Sanctuary throughout the year.

COVENANT OF THE GODDESS

P.O. Box 1226
Berkeley, CA 94701
Phone: N/A

One of the largest and oldest Wiccan religious organizations, the Covenant's members and practitioners are intent on reviving the practices of the pre-Christian Earth religion and adapting them to the twentieth century.

THE BEAR TRIBE MEDICINE SOCIETY
P.O. Box 9167
Spokane, WA 99209
Phone: (509) 326-6561

HUNA RETREATS, ALOHA INTERNATIONAL
P.O. Box 665
Kilauea, HI 96754
Phone: (808) 828-0302

THE SUNDANCE CEREMONY
The Deer Tribe Metis Medicine Society
11259 East Via Linda Street, 100-142
Scottsdale, AZ 85259
Phone: (602) 443-3851

SUFI CENTERS

THE SUFI ORDER OF THE WEST
P.O. Box 30065
Seattle, WA 98103
Phone: (206) 525-6992

To discover prayer, dance, and sound centers for the Islamic faith of Sufism, contact the Sufi Order of the West.

Naqshbandi

HAQQANI FOUNDATION MAIN CONVENTION AND RETREAT CENTER
7007 Fenton Hill Road
Fenton, MI 48430
Phone: (810) 629-4941

MAIN HOME OFFICE OF HAQQANI FOUNDATION
10933 Northcrest Lane
Los Altos Hills, CA 94024
Phone: (415) 941-7916   Fax: (415) 941-5047

JIHAD AL-AKBAR SO SATSU KEN DOJO
Linda Vista Drive
Mountain View, CA 94043
Phone: (415) 964-3656

MASJID AL-IMAN
4606 Martin Luther King Jr. Way
Oakland, CA 94609
Phone: N/A

HAQQANI ISLAMIC SUFI CENTER
North Pfingsten
Northbrook, IL 60062
Phone: (713) 267-7001

HAQQANI ISLAMIC SUFI CENTER
3023 West Belmont Avenue
Chicago, IL 60618
Phone: (312) 267-7001

HAQQANI ISLAMIC SUFI CENTER
2226 East 75th Street
Chicago, IL 60649
Phone: (312) 267-7001

NEW YORK HAQQANI FOUNDATION SUFI GATHERING CENTER
355 West 39th Street
New York, NY 10018
Phone: (212) 563-7302

WOODSTOCK SUFI CENTER
805 Zena Road
Woodstock, NY 12498
Phone: (914) 679-2933

CINCINNATI HAQQANI MOSQUE
724 West McMillan Street
Cincinnati, OH 45206
Phone: N/A

MINNEAPOLIS HAQQANI CENTER
712 5th Street NE
Minneapolis, MN 54413
Phone: (612) 331-3122

PHILADELPHIA HAQQANI DHIKR
250 East Wynnewood Road, #A25
Wynnewood, PA 19096
Phone: N/A

SEATTLE NAQSHBANDI DHIKR
9040 53rd Avenue South
Seattle, WA 98118
Phone: N/A

LOS ANGELES HAQQANI HOUSE
1802 North Sumner
Claremont, CA 91711
Phone: (909) 621-7777

SOLVANG SUFI GATHERINGS
Home of Ali Jensen
315 2nd Street
Solvang, CA 93463
Phone: (805) 688-4445

WASHINGTON, D.C. HAQQANI CENTER
1337 Ritchie Place NE
Washington, DC 20017
Phone: (202) 829-3303 or (703) 820-4342

THE "NATURAL HEALING" CREATIVE ARTS STUDIO
530 East Liberty Street, Suite 917
Ann Arbor, MI 48104-2210
Phone: (313) 930-9963   Fax: (313) 930-9832

DALLAS MASJID AL-HAQQ
2723 Alaska Avenue
Dallas, TX 75216
Phone: (214) 371-6390

Nimatullahi

306 West 11th Street
New York, NY 10014
Phone: (212) 924-7739

4931 MacArthur Boulevard NW
Washington, DC 20007
Phone: (202) 338-4757

84 Pembroke Street
Boston, MA 02118
Phone: (617) 536-0076

4021 19th Avenue
San Francisco, CA 94132
Phone: (415) 586-1313

11019 Arieta Avenue
Mission Hills, CA 91345
Phone: (818) 365-2226

219 Chace Street
Santa Cruz, CA 95060
Phone: (408) 425-8454

310 NE 57th Street
Seattle, WA 98105
Phone: (206) 527-5018

4642 North Hermitage
Chicago, IL 60640
Phone: (312) 561-1616

405 Greg Avenue
Santa Fe, NM 87501
Phone: (505) 983-8500

1784 Lawrence Avenue West
North York, Toronto, Ontario
Canada M6L 1E2
Phone: (416) 242-9397

GENERAL RESOURCE CENTERS

The following is a list of general resource centers that have some important connection to prayer and may therefore be useful.

ALBERT SCHWEITZER INSTITUTE FOR THE HUMANITIES

515 Sherman Avenue
Hamden, CT 06514
Phone: (203) 562-3039

This is a nonprofit, nonpartisan, nongovernmental institute affiliated with the United Nations and with a mission to sustain reverence for life by supporting educational, spiritual, and physical well-being within humanity and the environment. Programs include lectures, workshops, courses, awards—related to health care, religion, ethics, and human and animal rights.

ASSOCIATION OF PROFESSORS AND RESEARCHERS IN RELIGIOUS EDUCATION (APRRE)

10 Phillips Street
Medway, MA 02053
Phone: N/A

APRRE provides the magazine *Religious Education*, of which it is co-publisher, plus groups and courses related to adult education, technology, history of religious education, ethnography and other subjects. An annual meeting is held for members and associates.

AU SABLE INSTITUTE OF ENVIRONMENTAL STUDIES

7526 Sunset Trail NE
Mancelona, MI 49659
Phone: (616) 587-8686

This is a Christian environmental institute whose mission is to bring healing and wholeness to the environment and the world. It offers courses of study for students and Christian colleges. The institute is based in the Michigan forests, and the courses offer facilities for environmental stewardship at degree level with grants for study of environmental analysis, water and land resources analysis.

BUDDHIST PEACE FELLOWSHIPS
P.O. Box 4650
Berkeley, CA 94704
Phone: N/A

This fellowship is based on Buddhist beliefs in good relationships and nonviolence, and it publishes various magazines of interest.

FAITH AND VALUES CHANNEL
74 Trinity Place, 9th Floor
New York, NY 10006
Phone: (212) 964-1663
Toll-free: 1-800-841-8476

This is a 24-hour-a-day TV cable channel that offers programming to more than 20 million homes throughout America. The channel can be received through two satellite networks: the Vision Interfaith Satellite Network and the American Christian Television System. It links Catholic, Protestant, Jewish, Evangelical, and Eastern faiths and permits no fundraising or proselytizing. The channel's programs include documentaries, worship, prayer, drama, talk shows, music, and children's programs.

WORLD PEACE PRAYER SOCIETY
800 Third Avenue, 37th Floor
New York, NY 10022-7604
Phone: N/A

This is a member-supported nondenominational organization dedicated to raising peace consciousness through prayer and affirmation. It sponsors World Peace Prayer Ceremonies, the Peace Pole Project, the Peace Pals project for young people, and the Peace Message booklet campaign.

INTERNET PRAYER LINKS

There are many prayer and online ministry sites on the World Wide Web; I have listed a few starting on the opposite page. (These addresses were confirmed as of press time, but Web sites and addresses are constantly changing.) You can also use any of the Web search engines to find sites under listings such as "prayer," "prayer ministry," "meditation," "online prayer," and "online devotions."

You should always be cautious when signing on to any Web site; since the Internet is an open forum, there is enormous variation in the quality and substance of Web sites and pages. I have made every effort to ensure that the sites listed here are reputable, interesting, enlightening, and enjoyable.

You may know of special locations for prayer and worship that are not included in this or any of the other listings. Please write to me in care of the publisher about any unique places that you think should be included. We will add your suggestions when we revise the directory section for future editions of this book.

CHURCH OF GOD INTERNATIONAL OFFICES
E-mail: cog@chatt.mindspring.com

This prayer request link is designed to give you an opportunity to send your prayer requests to the Church of God International Offices. They will then be included in special prayer times and with the prayer group that meets every Wednesday morning in the chapel.

INTERNATIONAL INTERFAITH ORGANIZATION
Internet address: http://www.pacpub.com/sponsors/prayerl.html

The International Interfaith Organization is dedicated to the practice of prayer, meditation, and spirituality; of prayer, live prayers and archive of prayers; and the way of prayer. Talk with them—ask questions, chat, and send feedback via e-mail.

FIRST UNITED METHODIST CHURCH OF CRYSTAL LAKE
Internet address: http://gbgmumc.org/churches/CrystalLakeIL/prayer.html

Prayer requests or new participants can be put on the prayer chain by contacting the pastors. This ministry has teams of two in the Hale Chapel 30 minutes before, during, and 30 minutes after all worship services to pray for the pastors, congregation, and prayer requests received during the week.

E-PRAYER (CHRISTIAN)

E-mail: Webmaster@e-prayer.org

E-prayer, like many new services, was one borne of frustration. It was designed as a reminder to start each day in prayer.

THE UPPER ROOM LIVING PRAYER CENTER

P.O. Box 189

Nashville, TN 37202-0189

Internet address: http://www.upperroom.org

INTERNATIONAL LOCATIONS
FOR PRAYER

✌

The following are a few very choice locations for those traveling abroad in search of prayer. Although the United States does not lack prayerful locations, Europe and India (the areas from which the following locations have been chosen) have the benefit of ancient inheritances of the holy, some thousands of years old; and the following locations will bring the visitor instantly into a state of silence and meditation that is hard to achieve anywhere else in the world.

ITALY
The Roman Catholic Franciscan Church of Saint Francis of Assisi

The small, unique town of Assisi lies in the district of Umbria, which is east of Tuscany in Italy, between Florence and Rome. It is about a three hours' drive from Florence, through some of the most picturesque and glorious country in the world. By the time the visitor arrives at the edge of the town, which cannot be entered (except by residents) except on foot, the sense of divinity has already set in—as the land is already more sacred than most lands—and brings the heart, mind, and spirit into a state of calm.

Assisi itself is older than Christianity, but the town has been fashioned during the last several hundred years around one man—a Christian saint who lived in the thirteenth century and was permitted by the Roman Catholic pope of the time to set up his own church.

In the summer of 1224, Francis went to the mountain retreat of La Verna (Alvernia), not far from Assisi, to celebrate the feast of the Assumption of the Blessed Virgin Mary (August 15) and to prepare for Saint Michael's Day (September 29) by a 40-day fast. There he prayed that he might know how best to please God. Opening the Gospels for the answer, three times he came upon references to the Passion of Christ. As he prayed one morning, suddenly he beheld a figure coming toward him from the heights of heaven. Saint Bonaventure, general of the Franciscans from 1257 to 1274 and an important thinker of the thirteenth century, wrote:

> *As it stood above him, he saw that it was a man and yet a Seraph with six wings; his arms were extended and his feet conjoined, and his body was fixed to a cross. Two wings were raised above his head, two were extended as in flight, and two covered the whole body. The face was beautiful beyond all earthly beauty, and it smiled gently upon Francis. Conflicting emotions filled his heart, for though the vision brought great joy, the sight of the suffering and crucified figure stirred him to deepest sorrow. Pondering what this vision might mean, he finally understood that by God's providence he would be made like to the crucified Christ not by a bodily martyrdom but by conformity in mind and heart. Then as the vision disappeared, it left not only a greater ardor of love in the inner man but no less marvelously marked him outwardly with the stigmata of the Crucified.*

For the remainder of his life, Francis took the greatest care to hide the stigmata—marks resembling the wounds on the crucified body of Jesus Christ. After the death of Francis, Brother Elias announced the stigmata to the order by a circular letter. Later, Brother Leo, who was the confessor and intimate companion of the saint and who left a written testimony of the event, said that in death Francis seemed like one just taken down from the cross.

Francis lived two years longer, in constant pain and almost totally blind (he had contracted an eye disease in the East). Medical treatment was unsuccessful, and after a stay at Siena he was brought back to Assisi, where he died. He was buried temporarily in the church of San Giorgio, at Assisi. In 1230 his body was transferred to the lower church of the basilica that was being erected in his memory at the west end of the city.

The Church of Saint Francis is set in a deep square at the bottom end of the town, and in the crypt lie the relics of the saint and much silence and opportunity for prayer.

The Franciscan monks are evident throughout the town, with their brown habits, very often worn over jeans, some of them with guitars slung over their backs, which they will play to passersby in the streets of this exquisite location.

The Vatican, Rome

If you are serious about prayer and meditation, a visit to Italy is simply not complete without entering the Vatican. This is more than a church—it is an ecclesiastical state, seat of the Roman Catholic Church, and an enclave in Rome, situated on the west bank of the Tiber River. Its medieval and Renaissance walls form its boundaries except on the southeast at Saint Peter's Square (Piazza San Pietro). Of the six entrances, only three—the Piazza, the Arco delle Campane (Arch of the Bells) in the facade of Saint Peter's Basilica, and the entrance to the Vatican Museums in the north wall—are open to the public. Within the walls is a miniature nation. The most imposing building is Saint Peter's Basilica, built during the fourth century and rebuilt during the sixteenth century.

The city has its own telephone system, post office, and radio station as well as an army of more than 100 Swiss Guards, its own banking system and coinage, stores, and a pharmacy. Almost all supplies, including food, water, electricity, and gas, must be imported. There is no income tax and no restriction on the import or export of funds. Banking organizations and operations and expenditures are veiled in secrecy.

Vatican City's independent sovereignty was recognized by the then-Fascist Italian government in the Lateran Treaty of 1929. Sovereignty is exercised by the pope upon his election as the head of the Roman Catholic Church. He has absolute executive, legislative, and judicial powers within the city. The pope appoints the members of the Vatican's government organs, which are separate from those of the Holy See. The papal commission for Vatican City exercises the papal powers of government. Administrative powers are delegated to a governor, who is assisted by a central council.

The locations within the city of the Vatican that provide moments of silence and the opportunity for prayer are many and varied, and one of the guided tours is suggested to get to know what appeals for a second, "meditation visit."

ENGLAND
Saint Paul's Cathedral, London

Saint Paul's is the cathedral of the Church of England. The present
building was designed in a restrained, classical Baroque style by Sir
Christopher Wren and was constructed of Portland stone between
1675 and 1710, replacing Old Saint Paul's, which had been
completely destroyed in the Great Fire of 1666. As at Westminster
Abbey in London, many illustrious persons are buried in the main
body of the church and the crypt. The nearest tube (subway) station is
Saint Paul's, which is close to the city of London; so a walking tour
through the city is easy from here.

Westminster Abbey, London

Westminster Abbey (take the tube, or subway, to Westminster or
Victoria) was originally a Benedictine monastery, refounded as the
Collegiate Church of Saint Peter in Westminster (today one of the
boroughs constituting Greater London) by Queen Elizabeth I in 1560.
Legend relates that Sebert, the first Christian king of the East Saxons,
founded a church on a small Thames island—then known as Thorney
but later called the west minster, or monastery—and that this church
was miraculously consecrated by Saint Peter. It is certain that in about
785 C.E. there was a small community of monks on the island and
that the monastery was enlarged and remodeled by Saint Dunstan in
about 960 C.E..

Saint Edward the Confessor (reigned 1042–1066) built a new
church on the site, which was consecrated in 1065. It was of considerable size, cruciform in plan, and with a central and two western tow-
ers. In 1245 Henry III pulled down the whole of Edward's church
(except the nave) and replaced it with the present abbey church in the
pointed Gothic style of the period.

Since William the Conqueror, every British sovereign has been
crowned in the abbey except Edward V and Edward VIII, neither of
whom was crowned. Many kings and queens are buried near the
shrine of Edward the Confessor or in Henry VII's chapel. The last sovereign to be buried in the abbey was George II (died 1760); since then,
they have been buried at Windsor.

The abbey is also crowded with the tombs and memorials of famous British subjects. Part of the south transept is well-known as Poets' Corner, while the north transept has many memorials to British statesmen. The grave of the Unknown Warrior, whose remains were brought from Flanders in 1920, is in the center of the nave near the west door.

SPAIN
Santiago de Compostela, Galicia

The Church of Santiago de Compostela, of Galicia, northwestern Spain, is near the confluence of the Sar and Sarela Rivers, 32 miles southwest of La Coruña. *Santiago* is Spanish for "Saint James," whose shrine the city possesses. In 813 C.E. a tomb discovered at nearby Padrón was said to have been supernaturally revealed to be that of the apostle Saint James the Great, martyred at Jerusalem in about 44 C.E. His bones had been taken to Spain, where, according to legend, he had formerly evangelized. The discovery of the relics provided a rallying point for Christian Spain, then confined to a narrow strip at the north of the Iberian Peninsula, most of which was occupied by Moors. Over the tomb was built an earthen church that Alfonso III replaced by a stone one, and the town that grew up around it became the most important Christian place of pilgrimage after Jerusalem and Rome during the Middle Ages. The whole town, except the tomb itself, was destroyed and, in 1078, the present cathedral was rebuilt. This Romanesque building, located at the east end of the Plaza Mayor, has a Baroque west facade above a flight of steps. An outstanding feature of the interior is the Pórtico de la Gloria (located behind the facade), a tripartite porch showing the Last Judgment—Romanesque but tinged with Gothic features.

FRANCE
Notre Dame, Paris

Right in the center of Paris is the most famous of the Gothic cathedrals of the Middle Ages, distinguished for its size, antiquity, and archaeological as well as architectural interest. Maurice de Sully, bishop of Paris, conceived the idea of converting into a single building, on a larger scale, two earlier basilicas. The foundation stone was laid by Pope Alexander III in 1163, and the high altar was consecrated in 1189. The choir, west front, and nave were completed by 1240; and porches, chapels, and other embellishments were added over the next 100 years.

The cathedral suffered damage and deterioration through the centuries and had to be restored in the nineteenth century. The three great rose windows alone retain their thirteenth century glass. The flying buttresses of the apse are especially notable for their boldness and grace.

ISRAEL
Jerusalem

Jerusalem is the ancient city of the Middle East that, since 1967, has been wholly in the possession of Israel. Since 1949 the city has been claimed by Israel as its capital. Jerusalem has been inhabited since 1800 B.C. and is one of the principal holy places of the three great monotheistic faiths of Judaism, Christianity, and Islam. After the 1948 Arab-Israeli war, Jerusalem was divided between Transjordan (later Jordan), which annexed the Old City and the rest of East Jerusalem, and Israel, which held West Jerusalem. East Jerusalem was taken by Israel in the Six-Day War of 1967. Israel has declared Jerusalem to be its eternal and indivisible capital, and the status of the city has become a major point of contention between the Jewish state and its Arab neighbors.

Jerusalem is located near the center of Israel, about 15 miles west of the Dead Sea and 35 miles east of the Mediterranean Sea, in the watershed between the Mediterranean coastal plain and the Great Rift Valley of the Jordan River.

For Jews, Jerusalem is the repository of the holiest of memories, the focus of religious reverence and nationhood; for Christians, the scene of their savior's agony and triumph; and for Muslims, the goal of their prophet's mystic night journey and the site of the third most sacred shrine in Islam. The city was the capital of the ancient Hebrews and of their Jewish descendants until the first century C.E. During that century the city witnessed the ministry and crucifixion of Jesus Christ. The prophet Muhammad is believed by Muslims to have ascended to heaven from a site in Jerusalem.

Jerusalem's cultural climate is richly diverse. The Old City, still surrounded by a massive town wall from antiquity, contains Muslim, Jewish, Christian, and Armenian quarters. The Old City is dominated by the raised platform of the Herodian Temple Compound, the site of the First and Second Temples of the Hebrews and Jews. The compound includes the Islamic holy places of the Dome of the Rock and Al-Aqsa Mosque. Its Western (Wailing) Wall is the most sacred of Jewish shrines. The Old City is distinguished by its many churches and mosques and by the ancient synagogues and study houses of the Jewish Quarter.

Here is a whole city of prayerful locations, and a visitor can become almost punch-drunk with temples, churches, and mausoleums, each of which will satisfy the very greatest appetite for the holy and divine.

INDIA
The Kalighat Temple, Calcutta

The goddess Kali, in Hindu religious tradition, is one of the most important in India. There are many temples dedicated to her power and tradition, but one of the most impressive—and disturbing—is Kalighat Temple in Calcutta.

Kali in Sanskrit means "black"; in Hinduism, "a devouring, destructive goddess." In accordance with the Indian predilection for bringing together seemingly contradictory aspects of life, Kali is a fierce, terrifying aspect of Devi (the supreme goddess), who in other forms is represented as tranquil and pacific. Kali is depicted as a hideous, black-faced hag smeared with blood, with bared teeth and protruding tongue. Her four hands hold, variously, a sword, a shield, the severed hand of a giant, or a strangling noose; or they are stretched in a gesture of assurance. Kali is naked, except for her ornaments, consisting of a garland of skulls and a girdle of severed hands. In painting and in sculpture, she is often shown dancing on the inert body of her consort, Shiva.

Kali is said to have developed a taste for blood when she was called upon to kill the demon Raktavija, who produced 1,000 more like himself each time a drop of his blood fell on the earth. In order to vanquish him, she pierced him with a spear and, holding him high, drank his blood before it reached the ground. Goats are sacrificed to her daily at her temples, such as the Kalighat, in Calcutta. The thugs, assassins who operated in India until the nineteenth century, were worshipers of Kali and made ritual offerings of their victims to her.

All this may sound somewhat daunting for any visitor, but if you get the chance to go there, the experience of this extraordinary temple will be one of the most powerful and peaceful of your life.

Mount Abu

One of the most holy and meditative locations in the world, in southwestern Rajasthan state, northwestern India, is Mount Abu. The town is situated on the slopes of Mount Abu, an isolated feature of the Aravali Range. The city is a noted hill resort, and the Jaina temples at nearby Dilwara, built of white marble, are famous. Tejpal temple, built about 1200, is known for the delicacy and richness of its carvings, especially for that on the underside of its dome. The earlier Vimala Vasahi temple, built about 1031, is simpler and bolder in style.

The significance of Mount Abu itself is that it is regarded as a natural temple, and there are many courses and meditation camps that take place there. The visit is worthwhile just to feel the incredible simplicity and divinity of the location.

Taj Mahal

The Taj Mahal was built as a mausoleum on the southern bank of the Yamuna (Jumna) River, outside Agra in India. It was built by the Mughal emperor Shah Jahan in memory of his wife, Arjumand Banu Begam, also called Mumtaz Mahal ("Chosen One of the Palace"), of which the name Taj Mahal is a corruption. She died in childbirth in the town of Burhanpur in 1631 after having been the emperor's inseparable companion since their marriage in 1612. The building was commenced about 1632 and took more than 20,000 workers who were employed daily to complete the mausoleum itself 22 years later at a cost of 40 million rupees, an amount which would today translate to several hundred million U.S. dollars.

The whole complex was conceived and planned as an entity because Mughal building practice allowed no subsequent addition or amendment. Its northern end contains the most significant architecture, with mosque and jawab both facing the mausoleum.

The mausoleum itself, which stands on a marble plinth 23 feet high, has four identical facades with chamfered corners and a massive arch that rises to a height of 108 feet on each face. The Taj Mahal is regarded both as a supreme achievement of architecture and as one of the most beautiful buildings in the world. It contains an astonishingly deep atmosphere of silence and tranquillity. Facing it from the far end of the lake that stretches out before it is an experience that brings awe and almost shock at its beauty.

Sources for Part Two:
A Gathering of Prayers

ৎৢ

'Abdu'l-Bahá (1844–1921): Baha'i religious leader.

Amenhotep IV: King of Egypt (circa 1375–1358 B.C.E.) who rejected the old gods and initiated a new form of sun worship.

The Anima Christi: A prayer used in Christian celebrations and means "Soul of God or Christ."

Anselm, Saint (1033–1109): Italian-born English theologian, founder of Scholasticism.

Apocrypha: From the Book of Solomon, one of the books not included in the King James Version of the Bible.

Böhme, Jakob (1575–1624): German mystic whose works describe evil as a necessary antithesis to good. Also considered the founder of modern theosophy.

Carmichael, Amy (1868–1951): Missionary to Japan and India.

Chinmoy, Sri (contemporary): Born in Bengal in India in 1931, has dedicated his life since age 12 to the pursuit of peace and uplifting of the human spirit. Has established meditation centers around the world and written more than 1,100 books of poetry, plays, and songs. Founder of the Oneness-Home Peace Run, an annual peace run.

Desiderata: An anonymously written affirmation of ideal human behavior. The date is unknown but is probably the Middle Ages in England.

Devara Dasimayya (tenth century): Poet and mystic.

Donne, John (1572–1631): One of the greatest British poets.

Dunn, Philip (contemporary): Author and compiler of this book, and author of many books on religion, prophecy, and child care.

Eknath (1548–1600): Hindu poet and saint.

Emerson, Ralph Waldo (1803–1882): American lecturer, essayist, and poet. Leading Transcendentalist.

Ethical Fragment: A piece of inscribed holy scripture from one of the many remains or parchments found from ancient civilizations.

Farid ud-Din Attar (born between 1120 and 1157, died between 1193 and 1235): Persian Sufi poet. Educated as a theologian, after traveling widely, settled in his hometown but tried for heresy and banished.

Galgani, Saint Gemma (1878–1903): Perhaps one of the most beautiful of all women saints, both physically and spiritually.

Gibran, Kahlil (late nineteenth century): Middle Eastern mystic who wrote *The Prophet.*

Grand Pueblos: Mexican tribe.

Heracleitus (circa fourth century B.C.E.): Greek philosopher. Maintained that all things were in a state of flux and that fire was their origin. Known as the weeping philosopher because of his melancholy views on the changing character of life.

Hopkins, Gerard Manley (1844–1889): British poet known for many works published posthumously.

Housman, Alfred Edward (1859–1936): English scholar and celebrated poet.

Ignatius of Loyola, Saint (1491–1556): Spanish ecclesiastic who founded the Jesuits.

Inayat Khan, Hazrat (1882–1927): Indian Sufi born into a family of great musicians. Master musician at an early age and worked for revival of spiritual heritage in Indian music. Initiated into Sufism and trained in four major schools. At age 28, his training was complete and he left India for the West, lecturing extensively in Europe and the United States.

Juan de la Cruz (Saint John of the Cross) (1542–1591): Spanish priest who lived during the height of the Protestant Reformation's rebellion against the Catholic Church in northern Europe.

Kipling, Rudyard (1865–1936): English novelist, short-story writer, and poet.

Lao-tzu (circa sixth century B.C.E.): Chinese sage and founder of Taoism. Putative author of the Taoist classic *Tao Te Ching.*

Lathrop, Blessed Rose Hawthorne (1851–1926): Founder of the religious order of Dominican Servants of Relief for Incurable Cancer.

Lawrence, Brother (1605–1691): First a soldier, then a kitchen worker in monastic life, and finally a hermit.

Margaret of Cortona, Saint (1247–1297): Originally the mistress of a rich man, after his death, became a penitent worker for the poor.

Meeker, Nancy Rose (contemporary): American poet and author.

Mira Bai (circa 1498–1546): Indian noblewoman who married a prince, but her devotion to Krishna caused her to reject all conventional values. Leaving the women's quarters, she would mix with holy men and dance before the image in the temple. This flouting of social mores led to her persecution, including an attempt at poisoning.

Muktananda, Swami (1908–1982): Indian mystic.

Nachman of Bratzlav, Rabbi (1771–1811): Polish Hasidic teacher and storyteller.

Nanak, Guru (1469–circa 1539): The most honored of the ten Sikh gurus. He started out as an accountant but received God's call while bathing in the Bein River. Three days afterward, he gave away all his possessions and began to travel and teach.

Navajo: Native American tribe.

Neri, Saint Philip (1515–1595): A saint with a reputation for humor.

Niebuhr, Reinhold (1892–1971): An American theologian who wrote about Christianity's refusal to confront social ills.

Origen (185–254 C.E.): The most important theologian and biblical scholar of the early Greek period.

Paramahansa Yogananda (contemporary): Indian yogi and teacher.

Prisca, Saint (first century B.C.E.): Martyred saint during the Roman Empire.

Ptah-hotep (circa 2600 B.C.E.): Egyptian sage. Most ancient author known to us by name.

Rabi'a al-Adawiyya (717–801 C.E.): A saint of Islam and one of the central Sufi figures. She lived in Basra, now Iraq. Sold as a slave after her parents' death from famine, she later was freed and became a flute player. Lived always in poverty.

Ramakrishna, Shri (1836–1886): A religious genius of the nineteenth century, he experimented with virtually all the evolutionary paths and pronounced that all religions were directed toward the same God but used different paths. He was initiated into Tantric practices when 25 years old. He tried, "scientifically," to explain each stage in the ascent of the Kundalini; but each time he came to the penultimate Samadhi, he became lost to the outside world and would pass into unconsciousness.

Stevenson, Robert Louis (1850–1894): British poet and author.

Tagore, Rabindranath (1861–1941): Indian poet. Born in Calcutta, studied in London, returned to India where he founded a school, became India's most popular poet, won the Nobel prize for literature in 1913, knighted in 1915. Lectured worldwide and was in personal contact with renowned thinkers of his day from Europe and India. Wrote about 100 books of verse, about 50 plays, about 40 works of fiction, and about 15 books of essays.

Ten Bears: A Yamaparika Comanche Native American chieftain.

Tewa: Native American tribe.

Teresa of Avila, Saint (1515–1582): Spanish Carmelite nun.

Therese of Lisieux, Saint (1873–1897): Carmelite nun canonized in 1925.

White Eagle (White Eagle Trust): The White Eagle Trust was set up in England to administer and publish the works of White Eagle, an inspirational teacher, whose works include *The Quiet Mind* and various compilations of prayer. The White Eagle Trust is in Liss, Hampshire, England.

BIBLIOGRAPHY
AND READING LIST

The following books were used as source material for this book, plus a few more are of interest for further information about prayer and spiritual life.

An African Prayer Book. Desmond Tutu. Doubleday Books, New York.

Being Peace. Thich Nhat Hanh. Parallax Press, Berkeley, California.

The Bhagavad Gita. Translated by Juan Mascaro. Penguin Books, London; New York.

Blessings—Prayers for the Home and Family. Compiled by Rosemary Ellen Guiley. Pocket Books, New York.

The Book of Common Prayer. Cambridge University Press, Cambridge, England.

The Book of Mirdad. Mikhail Naimy. Arkana Penguin, New York; London.

The Buddhist Directory. Peter Lorie and Julie Foakes. Macmillan Publishing, London.

Celtic Devotional—Daily Prayers and Blessings. Caitlin Matthews. Harmony Books, New York.

Daily Meditations for Practicing the Course. Karen Casey. HarperCollins, New York; San Francisco.

The Dhammapada. Translated by Juan Mascaro. Penguin Books, London; New York.

Graces—Prayers and Poems for Everyday Meals and Special Occasions. June Cotner. HarperCollins, San Francisco.

Heart Songs—Everyday Prayers and Meditations. Sri Chinmoy. Hazelden, Center City, Minnesota.

Islam, Religion of Life. Abdul Wadod Shalabi. The Quilliam Press, Buckinghamshire, England.

Life Prayers—The Human Journey. Elizabeth Roberts and Elias Amidon. HarperCollins, San Francisco.

Meditation, The First and Last Freedom. Osho. St. Martin's Press, New York.

A Meditation Theme for Each Day. Hazrat Inayat Khan. Omega Publishing, New Lebanon, New York.

Metaphysical Meditations. Paramahansa Yogananda. The Self-Realization Fellowship, Los Angeles.

Native American Wisdom (of the *Classic Wisdom* series). Edited by Kent Nerburn and Louise Menglekoch. New World Library, San Rafael, California.

One Hundred Graces. Selected by Marcia and Jack Kelly. Bell Tower, Random House, New York.

Prayer in the New Age—A White Eagle Book of Prayer and Affirmation. The White Eagle Publishing Trust, Hampshire, England.

Prayer Is Good Medicine. Larry Dossey, M.D. HarperCollins, San Francisco.

Prayers for the Pilgrim Festivals, volumes 1 and 2. Polak and Van Gennep. Amsterdam.

Prayers of the Saints—An Inspired Collection of Holy Wisdom. Woodeene Koenig-Bricker. HarperCollins, San Francisco.

Remembrance, An Anthology of Readings, Prayers, and Music Chosen for Memorial Services. Introduced by Ned Sherrin. Michael Joseph, London.

Retreat—Time Apart for Silence and Solitude. Roger Housden. HarperCollins, San Francisco.

Rilke's Book of Hours—Love Poems to God. Translated by Anita Barrows and Joanna Macy. Riverhead Books, New York.

The Roaring Stream—A New Zen Reader. Edited by Nelson Foster and Jack Shoemaker. The Ecco Press, Hopewell, New Jersey.

Source Book for Earth's Community of Religions, revised edition. Edited by Joel D. Beversluis. CoNexus Press and Global Education Associates, Grand Rapids, Michigan.

365 Tao, Daily Meditations. Deng Ming-Dao. HarperCollins, San Francisco.

Traveling the Path of Love—Sayings of Sufi Masters. Edited by Llewwellyn Vaughan-Lee. The Golden Sufi Center, Inverness, California.

The Upanishads. Translated by Juan Mascaro. Penguin Books, London; New York.

The Voice of Kahlil Gibran, An Anthology. Edited by Robin Waterfield. Arkana Penguin, New York; London.

What Happens When Women Pray. Evelyn Christenson. Victor Books, Wheaton, Illinois.

Zen Words for the Heart—Hakuin's Commentary on the Heart Sutra. Translated by Norman Waddell. Shambhala Publications, Boston; London.

CREDITS

❧

ILLUSTRATIONS
Corbis-Bettmann: Pages 8, 11, 12, 15, 27, 34, 35, 38, 44, 48
Culver Pictures: Page 42
Ann Ronan/Image Select: Pages 3, 30, 46, 51

PHOTOGRAPHS
Corbis-Bettmann: Pages 31, 36, 37, 59, 63
Nadeem Naimy: Page 55
Reuters/Corbis-Bettmann: Page 10
Ann Ronan/Image Select: Page 19
UPI/Corbis-Bettmann: Page 39

FIRST-LINE PRAYER INDEX

KEY-WORD INDEX

❧